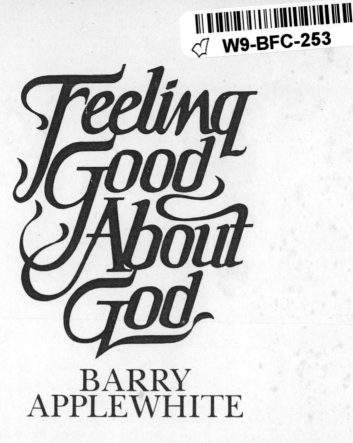

# Feeling Good About God

## BARRY APPLEWHITE

While this book is designed for the reader's personal enjoyment and profit, it is also intended for group study. A Leader's Guide with Victor Multiuse Transparency Masters is available from your local bookstore or from the publisher at $3.50.

**VICTOR BOOKS**

a division of SP Publications, Inc.
WHEATON, ILLINOIS 60187

*Offices also in* Fullerton, California • Whitby, Ontario, Canada • Amersham-on-the-Hill, Bucks, England

Most of the Scripture quotations in this book are from the *New International Version* (NIV), © 1978 by The New York International Bible Society. Other quotations are from the *King James Version* (KJV) and *The Living Bible* (LB), © 1971 by Tyndale House. All are used by permission of the publishers. Portions of Scripture are italicized by the author for emphases.

Recommended Dewey Decimal Classification: 231.4
Suggested Subject Heading: THE CHARACTER OF GOD; ATTRIBUTES OF GOD

Library of Congress Catalog Card Number: 81–50634
ISBN: 0–88207–339–7

VICTOR BOOKS
A division of SP Publications, Inc.
P.O. Box 1825 • Wheaton, Illinois 60187

# Contents

Introduction    **6**

1 The Answer Is a Person    **7**

2 Influencing God    **15**

3 Compassion without Compulsion    **26**

4 Encountering Life and Death    **36**

5 Power for a Change    **45**

6 The King of Heaven and Earth    **54**

7 God's Lavish Hand    **62**

8 The Ultimate Friend    **70**

9 The Unique Center of Life    **80**

10 Caring When It Hurts    **89**

11 The Accepter    **99**

12 The Exit Maker    **111**

To
Ken and Linda Bates
and
Frank and Kathy Wichern
who ski with me
and camp with me
and love me anyway!

# Acknowledgments

I deeply appreciate the people of Fellowship Bible Church in Dallas, Texas who have granted me the freedom to think about the Word of God without pressure to conform to familiar interpretations. I can identify with Paul's experience at Berea where "they received the message with great eagerness and examined the Scriptures every day to see if what Paul said was true" (Acts 17:11).

My warmest thanks to Mrs. Mary Lou McNevin and Miss Mary Quinette in using their typing talents for this book.

# Introduction

I think I can help you understand this book better by telling you why I wrote it as I did.

First, I wanted to show how God's character *relates directly to our everyday lives*. So I have used actual incidents from the lives of biblical characters to isolate the practical significance of God's personality. As you see His dynamic involvement with Moses, Abraham, Daniel, and others, you will get concrete ideas about what He is doing (and what He wants to do) in your life. The personal applications at the end of each chapter will help you integrate what you have learned into your daily experience.

Second, I wanted to enhance your understanding of God as a *Person* who cares about you. So often believers think of God as aloof and uncaring rather than directly interacting with us in a personal way. Perhaps I can capture the difference with a question: Would you rather relate to a perfect Sovereign or a loving Father? I find the latter more appealing and I'll try to show that an emphasis on the loving Father represents the biblical view.

Third, I wanted to devote most of the chapters to incidents from the Old Testament because I feel the riches there have been largely untapped by today's believers. I hope to refresh your interest in the Old Testament by shedding new light on some familiar stories.

Finally, I urge you to read every biblical passage in the book carefully before reading my comments on them. Otherwise you will be constantly looking back to understand what I'm writing about. As always, letting God speak first puts man's ideas in proper perspective.

# 1
# The Answer Is
# a Person

## God Is Personal

Looking back at my college years, I wonder how I could have been an "A" student and taken so long to catch on. People even told me that I should be asking myself the *big* questions: "Who am I? What does my life mean?" Frankly, such suggestions puzzled me. I wasn't asking such questions at all. I considered it silly and pointless because I already had the answers.

"Who am I?" Mentally I replied: "I'm Barry Applewhite, the son of Paul and Mona Applewhite, a Texan, a lover of sports, astronomy, and chess." You see, I knew who I was.

"What does my life mean?" That was simple too! In high school and college it meant making good grades. After college, life would mean succeeding in my profession. No mystery there either.

Obviously my answers had all the depth of a rain puddle, but they satisfied me for a long time. I didn't even begin to come up with better responses until I became a Christian in my senior year at college. Only after entering into a relationship with Jesus Christ did I find new and better answers to my most basic needs.

With hindsight I have forgiven myself for being so naive about spiritual truth during those years. Now I realize that a person can't really know who he is and what life means until he knows God. Finding out who God is sharpened my search for life's meaning like looking at the picture on a puzzle box.

It comforted me to learn that Moses didn't solve his life-puzzle until he was 80 years old. He gained knowledge of God in a most unlikely place—the desert of Sinai. In our culture Moses would have the educational equivalent of a double doctorate. And yet the Bible portrays him at 80 tending sheep in the middle of nowhere. That's not how things are supposed to work!

As a brilliant man living out a seemingly trivial life, I suspect Moses spent long hours wondering, "Who am I and what does my life mean?" The Hebrews felt that the wilderness was fit only for outcasts—the rejects of society. How did Moses get there? Joseph (Moses' ancestor) had died about 350 years earlier and his people had been reduced to slavery in Egypt. After Moses' miraculous upbringing in Pharaoh's palace, he had committed murder in a misguided attempt to deliver his people. He fled to the desert to escape a death sentence. He had 40 long years to ponder his aborted life as an outcast murderer from a slave race.

Like Moses, the Israelites had ample reason to question their identity and purpose. As one oppressive year followed another, they gradually forgot about the Lord. Only by understanding the trials and doubts of Moses and his people can we grasp their defeated and resistant attitudes. They had never read the Book of Exodus! The Israelites faced a crisis of identity and purpose similar to what individuals face. God's answer for their needs will meet our's too.

# The Sign

Now Moses was tending the flock of Jethro his father-in-law, the priest of Midian, and he led the flock to the far side of the desert and came to Horeb, the mountain of God. There the angel of the Lord appeared to him in flames of fire from within a bush. Moses saw that though the bush was on fire it did not burn up. So Moses thought, "I will go over and see this strange sight—why the bush does not burn up" (Ex. 3:1-3).

*We* know that the bush was burning because of the angel of the Lord, but Moses saw only a bush aflame. Moses knew nothing of this miracle just as he did not see the quiet ways God had been working during the long years of Hebrew slavery. As the Pharaohs had increased the people's hardships, God had caused the population to multiply even faster. Even Moses' name (meaning "one drawn out") implied God's purpose that Moses would one day lead the people out of slavery. Moses led the sheep of his flock to the mountain of God just as he would later lead God's flock to the same place. These evidences of God's work were hidden from Moses.

As we face crises in our own lives, it may appear to us (as it did to Moses) that God has been working somewhere else in His kingdom. We may even feel anger at His apparent absence, but our sight in such matters can fail. God had been secretly involved in Moses' life although he would not realize it until later.

## The Mission

When the Lord saw that he had gone over to look, God called to him from within the bush, "Moses, Moses!"

And Moses said, "Here I am."

"Do not come any closer," God said. "Take off your sandals, for the place where you are standing is holy ground." Then He said, "I am the God of your father, the God of Abraham, the God of Isaac, and the God of Jacob." At this, Moses hid his face, because he was afraid to look at God.

The Lord said, "I have indeed seen the misery of My people in Egypt. I have heard them crying out because of their slave drivers, and I am concerned about their sufferings. So I have come down to rescue them from the hand of the Egyptians and to bring them up out of that land into a good and spacious land, a land flowing with milk and honey—the home of the Canaanites, Hittites, Amorites, Perizzites, Hivites and Jebusites. And now the cry of the Israelites has reached Me, and I have seen the way the Egyptians are oppressing them. So now, go. I am sending you to Pharaoh to bring My people the Israelites out of Egypt" (Ex. 3:4-10).

When Moses approached, God called him by name and warned him to keep his distance from the bush. I think the Lord had a reason for this warning which also explains why Moses hid his face in fear. (Fear arises from an actual and powerful threat to a person's well-being.) As the Speaker revealed His identity, I think the flaming bush was transformed into the same towering inferno of fire that would later lead Israel. Moses hid in fear for his life.

While Moses quivers in fear, the Lord answers the nagging question of those bitter years. In saying, "I have *indeed seen* the misery of My people" (Ex. 3:7), God uses a Hebrew construction that intensifies the statement. The implied meaning is, "I have seen their misery with the result that I'm doing something about it."

The *New International Version* translates God's response to His people's needs in words which make Him sound like a state department bureaucrat: "I am *concerned* about their suffering" (Ex. 3:7). The Hebrew verb means to know something by experience. Since God has emotions, He *felt* their pain. He hurt because they hurt. In the same way, God feels our struggles intimately though we may think of Him as far removed from them.

The Lord states His intent to rescue the people from Egyptian oppression. But all this serves as a prelude to an order that shocked Moses to the core. God tells him to go and bring the people out. At that moment Moses' identity and purpose began to take shape

## The Objections and the Answer

But Moses said to God, "Who am I, that I should go to Pharaoh and bring the Israelites out of Egypt?"

And God said, "I will be with you. And this will be the sign to you that it is I who have sent you: When you have brought the people out of Egypt, you will worship God on this mountain."

Moses said to God, "Suppose I go to the Israelites and say to them, 'The God of your fathers has sent me to you,' and they ask me, 'What is His name?' Then what shall I tell them?"

God said to Moses, "I am who I am. This is what you are to say to the Israelites: 'I AM has sent me to you' " (Ex. 3:11-14).

Moses had seen this movie before and he didn't want a rerun. In his first attempt to deliver the people, his help was flatly rejected (Ex. 2:11-15). He had barely escaped execution and now God wanted him to walk right back into the same trap. Moses could look back over three centuries and see no assurance that the Lord would act decisively to back him up. He knew nothing of the great plagues and miracles to come. So Moses wonders out loud about his adequacy for the task: "Who am I?" (Ex. 3:11)

Do you ever feel like Moses did? Do you ever feel unequal to your God-appointed mission as a life-manager for Christ? Or unable to love your wife as Christ loves the church? I experience such feelings of inadequacy in my own life. I wonder how God can entrust a significant part of our church's spiritual growth to a mere man—me!

God's answer for Moses has profound implications for each one of us. In response to all of his doubts, fears, and questions, God simply says, *"I will be with you"* (v. 12). The answer to his needs is a Person! The Lord goes totally beyond the answers which human reason would have offered Moses. He doesn't explain how carefully Moses had been prepared for this task. He discloses nothing of His secret actions behind the scenes or of His plans for delivering the people. God assures a man filled with doubts and fears that He will stand with him in the crisis.

As we face trials and experience doubts, God offers us the same response. We find our answers in a Person who will be with us as we face opposition and feel the pressures of uncertainty.

Moses raised a second objection (v. 13). He knew the attitude he could expect from the Israelites. They would be skeptical and unbelieving. In effect they would say, "Sure, Moses, God has appeared to you. And if you believe *that*, we have some swamp land in the Nile Delta region we would like to sell you." The people would demand to know more about this God by learning His name. Moses may have been putting his own doubts into the mouth of the people because the Lord responded to the objection as if it belonged to Moses.

The Israelites believed that a name expressed something's essential nature or character. God's personal name occurs over 7,000 times in the Old Testament, but only here is it explained. Moses must say to the people, "I AM has sent me to you" (v. 14).

The Lord's name asserts two things: He is a Person (not a force, or an idea, or a thing) and, He is always living (not alive once-upon-a-time or for a limited time). As a *Person* ("I") He cares about us, interacts with us, and has a purpose for us. As the *living* God ("AM") His power and presence never falter while the years pass.

This ever-living Person said to Moses, "I will be with you." I believe that God has the same answer for each of us as believers. He doesn't tell us what to expect next in our lives and He gives no assurance that He will sweep our problems away with a stroke of His hand. He promises us Himself. We find *our* true identity and meaning in relationship to Him.

In the time of the patriarchs we read of the Creator—God *over* us. In the time of the Exodus we learn of God *with* us. We who have trusted Jesus Christ enjoy something more than Moses had—God *in* us. That's how intimately involved He is. God's answer to our needs is *still* a Person.

## How the Living God Relates to You

Use the following applicational concepts to evaluate your own life.

1. Just like Moses, *you have a purpose to accomplish for God.* Paul tells us that every believer is to "live a life worthy of the Lord" (Col. 1:10). But like Moses we sometimes drag our feet by raising objections and presenting problems to God. How would you react to the following statements?

- Generally speaking, I know what God wants of me and I'm seeking to do it.

    ☐ Yes    ☐ No    ☐ Not sure

- I have an adequate idea of what God wants of me, but I'm putting Him off with objections and problems.

    ☐ Yes    ☐ No    ☐ Not sure

- I think my life reflects the fact that God has a reason for my life; I have a purpose in life.

    ☐ Yes    ☐ No    ☐ Not sure

*Action Step*: You may find it necessary to clear up some of these issues by prayer, interaction with other believers, and study of the Bible.

2. Just like Moses, *you have to contend with doubt and conflict.* God says to us, "I AM" and "I will be with you." He doesn't remove all conflict or tell us all that will happen, but the living Lord promises us His presence. Can you identify with these statements?

- Sometimes I think that because I have problems, God is not with me. I feel empty and abandoned.
- Sometimes I think that because I have doubts, God wants nothing to do with me. I feel guilty and I despair of ever being free from doubt.

But even with doubt and conflict in your life, "God has said, 'Never will I leave you; never will I forsake you' " (Heb. 13:5).

*Action Step*: Have feelings of doubt and abandonment caused you to stop praying? Why not start again now?

## A Final Word

My favorite radio talk show leader is Barry Farber. At the end of his show he always says, "Keep asking questions."

It's important to keep asking questions in life, but eventually you must come up with some answers. I've found my answers. The naive ones of my college years have fallen away.

"Who am I?" I am a man who through faith in Christ can call God "Father." "What does my life mean?" It means living for Christ in all that I do. At last I have answers which will stand the test of time and eternity.

# 2
# Influencing God

## God Is Active

Do you ever have trouble giving God His proper place in your life? I know I do. Many factors can contribute to this, so let's explore a few.

Sometimes people harbor the thought that God cannot fully grasp the complexity of modern life. They see Him as the unenlightened God of long ago. To show how common this idea is, J. B. Phillips surveyed some British teenagers. He asked them to give an immediate answer to this question: "Can God understand radar?" Phillips reported that almost every person said "No!" and then laughed as they realized how absurd that was. ( From *Your God is Too Small*, Epworth Press, London, p. 18.)

I think each of us hides a degree of this doubt about God. Or perhaps we see the Lord as too holy and aloof to want involvement with us. Isn't God repulsed by our sins? Wouldn't He prefer the role of distant Sovereign to that of loving Father?

Or if God has already determined all events, then He doesn't need to relate to us. Our lives can simply just go on according to Plan.

But the main reason we don't always give God His proper place has not yet been mentioned. We're afraid of what He might do if we granted Him a free hand over our affairs. We prefer a God who is like an electric blanket on a cold winter night—a warm Person who can be adjusted to suit our needs, or even turned on and off. We secretly want a God who responds to *our* control, who is subject to *our* will.

In feeling this way we are experiencing a long-standing problem. As the Israelites escaped from their slavery in Egypt, they too found it difficult to submit to the Lord. They wanted to remake Him according to their own desires. They sought a God who would not make demands, charges, and threats. As Exodus 32 unfolds, we will see how Israel tried to alter the living God to fit into their schemes of life!

## The Road to Sinai

Before considering how the people tried to bring God into a docile form, let's review the historical setting of Exodus 32. A few months earlier God had delivered the nation out of oppressive slavery in Egypt. No sooner had the people come out than they faced extermination by the Egyptian army on the west shore of the Red Sea. They were trapped! But God parted the sea and destroyed the would-be destroyers. With the Lord's power Israel later beat off the Amalekites. During the long march to Mt. Sinai, God worked daily miracles to feed over two million people in the midst of desolation. All of these mighty events occurred just days before their arrival at Mt. Sinai.

Soon after the people made camp, God descended upon the mountain in a terrifying cloud of smoke and fire. A great earthquake ripped the ground out from under their feet! This caused the people to have a new and powerful fear of the Lord. They swore to keep all God's laws. So Moses ascended the mountain to receive the covenant tablets from the Lord.

# A Custom-Made God

When the people saw that Moses was so long in coming
down from the mountain, they gathered around Aaron
and said, "Come, make us gods who will go before us.
As for this fellow Moses who brought us up out of
Egypt, we don't know what has happened to him" (Ex.
32:1).

As time passed, the people grew restless. Accustomed to the
column of fire and cloud towering over them, they no longer feared
God's nearness. But they could plainly see He was still there. We
can appreciate the depth of Israel's subsequent sin only by re-
membering what God had previously done and by realizing His
visible presence near the camp.

The Hebrew text makes it clear that the people gathered
"against" Aaron to put pressure on him. They spoke to him with
commands showing who was boss. They had tired of waiting and
wanted a god to escort them into Canaan immediately! In treating
Aaron as their leader, the people betrayed their true intentions.
They wanted a weak leader who could be bent to their will. They
disavowed Moses because *he* took charge.

This exchange of a strong leader for a weak one on the human
level conformed precisely to what they wanted on the divine level
as well. They wanted to replace their awesome and powerful God
with an impotent idol. And like Aaron, the idol would not interfere
with them. Such a god could be put in his place.

Aaron answered them, "Take off the gold earrings that
your wives, your sons and your daughters are wearing,
and bring them to me." So all the people took off their
earrings and brought them to Aaron. He took what they
handed him and made it into an idol cast in the shape of a
calf, fashioning it with a tool. Then they said, "These
are your gods, O Israel, who brought you up out of
Egypt."

When Aaron saw this, he built an altar in front of the calf and announced, "Tomorrow there will be a festival to the Lord." So the next day the people rose early and sacrificed burnt offerings and presented fellowship offerings. Afterward they sat down to eat and drink and got up to indulge in revelry (Ex. 32:2-6).

You may wonder how former slaves had possessed so much gold. They had received it from the Egyptians through the Lord's power (Ex. 12:35-36). Gold obtained for them by their powerful God was now used by them to make a powerless god. Aaron fashioned a young bull, imitating a common fertility god in both the Nile Delta and Canaan. The people had doubtless seen such gods being worshiped during their years of slavery in Goshen (Ex. 8:22), which was located in the Nile Delta. Fertility gods were often worshiped through *public* acts of sexual intercourse. Such scenes had been burned into the minds of the people.

With colossal self-deception the Israelites ascribed God's Exodus miracles to the bull Aaron had just made by hand! Isaiah heaps scorn on such idol makers (Isa. 44:16-17) by telling of one who carved his god out of half a log and then cooked his dinner over the other half! But we can understand such delusion when we admit that people want a god they can control—one who will not interfere with them. Such ideas are the roots of self-deception.

Aaron affirmed the people's fantasy by building an altar and proclaiming a festival (Ex. 32:5). Their sin did not occur impulsively. They had slept on their decision and then arose with enthusiasm "to indulge in revelry" (v. 6).This polite translation obscures the true nature of the festival. The Hebrew verb implies casual, public acts of a sexual nature. The people are worshiping their fertility god in the customary way! Just ahead of them looms the awesome mountain ablaze with fire (Deut. 9:15) while they willfully break the first and second commandments (Ex. 20:1-6). Just as Paul states in Romans 1, and just as we see in contemporary

American culture, people who fashion gods of their own liking often wind up in sexual immorality.

## Can a Man Influence God?

Then the Lord said to Moses, "Go down, because your people, whom you brought up out of Egypt, have become corrupt. They have been quick to turn away from what I commanded them and have made themselves an idol cast in the shape of a calf. They have bowed down to it and sacrificed to it and have said, 'These are your gods, O Israel, who brought you up out of Egypt.'

"I have seen these people," the Lord said to Moses, "and they are a stiff-necked people. Now leave Me alone so that my anger may burn against them and that I may destroy them. Then I will make you into a great nation" (Ex. 32:7-10).

It shouldn't surprise us that God felt intense anger at the intentional, public sin in which the Israelites were engaged in on the plain below. The words "go down" in verse 7 translate a double command ("go, go down") which is terse and abrupt in Hebrew. The text wreaks with God's rising anger! Moses had probably been scheduled to descend on the very day of the idol festival because the tablets had been completed (Ex. 31:18). God's fingers finished the tablets of His Law as Aaron's fashioned the bull!

The Lord related a conclusion, a decision, and a plan to Moses. He had concluded that the people were "stiff-necked" (Ex. 32:9), an image from the agricultural environment of Egypt. A farmer would direct his plowing ox to turn around. But a stiff-necked ox would ignore the turn signal. Thus "stiff-necked" means self-willed and stubborn. The people knew what direction God wanted, but they had ideas of their own.

In view of their blatant rebellion, the Lord decided to destroy them. He told Moses to stand aside so that "My anger may burn against them'' (v. 10). He's not talking about *becoming* angry; He *is* angry! For the Lord's anger to "burn against" the nation means that the people will actually experience it in judgment. Their abominable crime called for extreme judgment—death. Undoubtedly, the Lord would spare a few righteous people such as Moses. Through him God planned to make "a great nation" (v. 10).

Some scholars think that God's stated plan was just a trick. They suggest Moses was being tested for some hidden purpose. On the contrary, I believe God was 100 percent serious. The Lord had clear grounds for this judgment in the willful sin of the people. He would simply begin again with Moses as He had generations before with Noah. To say that God didn't intend to do what He said is to say He's not true to His word. This would be an assumption foreign to the text.

We expect to read next that Moses stepped aside while God destroyed Israel and then made him into a great nation (vv. 10ff). But such expectations get a mind-boggling shock. Moses intervenes with the Lord in one of the Bible's most pivotal intercessory passages.

> But Moses sought the favor of the Lord his God. "O Lord," he said, "why should Your anger burn against Your people, whom You brought out of Egypt with great power and a mighty hand? Why should the Egyptians say, 'It was with evil intent that He brought them out, to kill them in the mountains and to wipe them off the face of the earth'? Turn from Your fierce anger; relent and do not bring disaster on Your people. Remember Your servants Abraham, Isaac, and Israel, to whom You swore by Your own self: 'I will make Your descendants as numerous as the stars in the sky and I will give Your descendants all this land I promised them, and it will be their inheritance forever.' " Then the Lord relented and

did not bring on His people the disaster He had threatened (Ex. 32:11-14).

God was willing to be influenced by a person! He changed a completely justifiable course of action because of the prayer of a single man. Do you realize what that means? God does not allow us to control Him (as the Israelites could control their idol), but *He does permit us to influence Him.* We affect the Lord's actions by our prayers and by the ways in which we live.

God *dynamically interacted* with Moses about what would be done. The text gives no evidence at all of the Lord reversing His actions because He had long ago planned it that way. Rather it pictures God being influenced by the prayer of a righteous man. Take a look at James' words: "The prayer of a righteous man is powerful and effective" (James 5:16).

To understand Moses' prayer, we will examine each of his three arguments. He didn't present a single compelling plea! In spite of this, Moses made the best possible case in his prayer.

Paraphrasing Moses' first point (Ex. 32:11) we get this question: "Why destroy Your people after all the effort You made to bring them out? What a waste!" All God's Exodus miracles will go down the drain if He wipes out the nation. This is a good point—but not a decisive one.

Moses' second argument in verse 12 had a similar lack of force. If God executed the people, the Egyptians would blaspheme Him as having been evil from the start. Another good try, but not a compelling one. After all, people misunderstand and defame the Lord every day. That would hardly be a new experience for Him.

Finally, Moses seems to say that some would conclude God had broken His promise to Abraham, Isaac, and Israel. Moses knows that he is a descendant of these three. God would *not* break His promise in any way by rebuilding the nation through Moses. But someone might accuse the Lord of hiding in a covenant loophole. Give Moses credit! He makes the best possible case, but none of his arguments are sufficient to force the answer. (Some people who read this passage get the idea that Moses was reminding God of something He had forgotten in His anger. Others wrongly think Moses helped the Lord regain control after a temper fit! Rather, God has the freedom to carry out His threat, but He is also free to be influenced.)

Moses was righteous, *not* sinless. In fact, in chapter 1 we saw him arguing with God. Late in his life he lost the privilege of entering Canaan because of disobedience. But the prayer of a righteous man can affect the Lord! There *is* a way of life that pleases God. As we live that way, our clout with the Lord increases. We can't control, refashion, or compel Him, but we can influence Him by our actions and prayers.

I find this one of the most hopeful incidents in the Bible. God wants to interact with me and He really listens when I pray.

To confirm this picture of God "relenting," consider the words of the Lord found in Jeremiah 18:7-10. If He announces judgment on a nation and they turn away from evil, then the Lord will relent and withhold the judgment. God will also reconsider announced blessing if the nation sins. God's Word shows that He dynamically interacts with people according to clear principles. All future events are *not* already decreed in minute detail. God acts spontaneously while remaining true to His principles and considering our actions and prayers. That's why we need to pray!

## He Still Listens and Acts

Recently I heard Charles Colson, the former assistant to President Nixon, tell of a profound answer to prayer. Colson had tried for days to use his old Washington, D.C. contacts to get approval for a plan. He wanted to take certain Christian prisoners *out* of federal prisons, train them for two weeks, and then send them back in to build Christian fellowships. He got nowhere with this plan.

Finally, Colson visited the director of the Federal Bureau of

Prisons who politely listened to him. When Colson finished the director asked a question, but not about Colson's proposal. It seems that on a recent visit to a federal prison in California, the director had attended one of their chapel services. It totally astounded him to hear one of the prisoners pray for him and his wife. The director wanted Colson to tell him how a man could pray for someone who was keeping him in prison. Colson gave him a brief explanation of the Christian principles which led the prisoner to pray for his jailer. A short time later the director unexpectedly approved Colson's plan for training prisoners. Colson was convinced that this allshappened because *one* Christian prisoner prayed. (This story also appears in *Life Sentence*, by Charles W. Colson, Chosen Books, chap. 3.)

You may not be able to see yourself praying with the power of a Moses, but can you pray with the power of a prisoner? Why not try?

## Are You Making a God or Influencing God?

Use these ideas to help you evaluate your relationship to the Lord.

1. Many modern people are too sophisticated to craft golden idols as their gods. But like Israel we may have unique ways of trying to remake the one true God into gods that fit our fancies. Can you identify with any of these methods?

- I don't feel any need for God. I can live quite well without His help. I can determine my own destiny.
  (Core idea: *God can be safely ignored.*)

At some times in life *men* are more susceptible to this trap than at others. Daniel Levinson describes one such period in his scholarly study of male adult development (*The Seasons of a Man's Life,* Knopf, p. 60). Between age 36 and 41 men pass through a phase known as "becoming-one's-own-man." In this period a man becomes a senior member of work and society. He speaks more clearly with his own voice and enjoys an increasing measure of authority. He becomes less and less dependent upon other people and institutions. The big spiritual danger lies in a man extending these normal developments by one fatal step: "I don't need God anymore." A rising sense of autonomy can reduce a person's felt need for God. Has such a thing happened to you, your mate, or a friend?

- I don't want God to interfere in my life or my moral choices. I just leave Him alone and expect He will leave me alone.

  (Core idea: *God will not act against my will*.)

- I have my own special beliefs about God. I have a right to believe what I want to about Him.

  (Core idea: *God has to respect the sincerity of my ideas*.)

Some Christians and non-Christians have reached the conclusion that all *sincere* ideas about God are OK. Such reasoning reminds me of a song my five-year-old daughter made up one night on the way to church. She quietly sang, "I know everything, and 2 + 2 is 5." She was completely sincere and totally wrong!

A typically evangelical distortion of God often pictures Him as serenely uninvolved in human affairs.

- I am only living out a set plan of God's making. Every act of my life occurs through God's decree.

  (Core idea: *God does not interact with man*. His Plan simply unfolds.

Such a view runs into stiff opposition from the dynamic thrust of all biblical history. Moses had the audacity to appeal to God without concern for any plan. The Lord spontaneously responded!

2. God grants us an awesome tool to change our lives through prayer. He can be influenced by both our lives and our prayers! I would encourage you to set two goals for this week.

*Goal one*: I will pray more because I see that God really listens and is moved by prayer.

☐ Yes      ☐ No

On many occasions I have admitted from the pulpit that I don't pray as much as I should. (I know that's heresy for a pastor, but it has been the fact of my life.) I tend to feel self-sufficient. But as I studied and worked through chapter 32 of Exodus, the dynamic power of prayer finally got through to me. God actually listens and interacts with my life because of prayer. I began to pray daily for some friends on vacation who needed to have a good experience together. For me that was a drastic change! You can do it too.

*Goal two*: I will seek to live a life that pleases God because that influences His actions toward me.

☐ Yes        ☐ No

# 3
# Compassion without Compulsion

## God Is Free

Not long ago I did some time in jail. Fortunately, it was just two hours. But I stayed long enough to learn a vital lesson: I had been taking my freedom for granted.

As the time ended, I could choose to leave but the prisoner I visited could not. Still, I felt funny standing behind bars and knowing that my departure depended upon the guard opening the door. He had control over my freedom.

Think for a moment about the dozens of decisions you have made in the past six hours. Even life's simplest tasks require a constant process of choices. (For example, didn't you just unconsciously decide to read on?) We use freedom so much that only by losing it for a time can we grasp its extent and importance.

I believe that this common freedom relates directly to God. The Lord has desires, plans, and motives which lead Him to decide and act. His freedom interacts in a complex way with ours, and each of us has probably wondered about the degree to which our freedom is under His control.

The Scriptures give us hundreds of glimpses at the relationships between God's freedom and ours. However, this issue has generated controversy for centuries. God has apparently granted enough freedom for spiritually-minded people to reach different views! My own view will emerge as we look at another incident from Moses' life.

## God Steps Away

In the wake of the golden calf incident (see chap. 2), God drew back from contact with Israel, still encamped near Mt. Sinai. The Lord promised that His "angel" would lead the people into Canaan (Ex. 32:34), but He would not *personally* go with them. This withdrawal had a gracious motivation. Another great sin might provoke Him to destroy them (Ex. 33:3). Upon hearing this news, the people began to express remorse and repentance. Meanwhile, the Lord was deciding what to do with them (Ex. 33:5).

In this hour of decision, Moses exercised his freedom to press for God's full restoration of His presence and blessing to Israel.

## Moses Seeks Another Chance

Moses said to the Lord, "You have been telling me, 'Lead these people,' but You have not let me know whom You will send with me. You have said, 'I know you by name and you have found favor with Me.' If I have found favor in Your eyes, teach me Your ways so I may know You and continue to find favor with You. Remember that this nation is Your people" (Ex. 33:12-13).

As Moses made his first request, he based it on what the Lord had said. God's command to "lead these people" (v. 12) probably meant to take them into Canaan. After acknowledging this God-given mission, Moses draws attention to his special relationship with the Lord. For God to know someone "by name" (v. 12) implies a personal and intimate bond.

In between these statements Moses says, "You have not let me know whom You will send with me" (v. 12). That sounds strange because he seemingly ignores God's words about sending His angel (32:34). Moses was fudging a bit; he was expressing discontent with the revised plan. In effect Moses said, "I don't want some angel—I want You!" Moses kept pounding away at this basic request until God granted it.

In fact, this entire incident hinged around one main issue: Would the Lord restore a *full and complete* relationship with Israel or not? That's why Moses mentioned "the people" so frequently. When the Lord agreed to remake the broken convenant (Ex. 33:17), then Moses dropped this whole subject like a hot rock.

Moses was using his freedom most lovingly. He could have taken God's offer to start a new nation descending from him (see chap. 2). Instead he chose to intercede on behalf of others. His compassionate use of freedom had been well-learned from the Lord's example.

Moses named his two basic desires in verse 13: (1) "Teach me Your ways"; and (2) "Remember that this nation is Your people." Moses' second request again puts the people in the forefront. To understand this request it helps to recall that no part of the Bible yet existed. The only written revelation about God had been engraved on the two stone tablets that Moses shattered when he saw the golden calf. Moses asked God to rewrite His Law and thus restore His covenant with Israel. Only by following God's ways could Moses and the people be certain of future favor. This interpretation is confirmed by the fact that the Lord soon engraved new tablets as Moses suggested (Ex. 34:1-28).

## Two Concessions from God

The Lord replied, "My Presence will go with [them], and I will give you rest." Then Moses said to Him, "If Your Presence does not go with [them], do not send us up from here. How will anyone know that You are pleased with me and with Your people unless You go with us? What else will distinguish me and Your people from all other people on the face of the earth?'' And the Lord said to Moses, ''I will do the very thing you have asked, because I am pleased with you and I know you by name'' (Ex. 33:14-17).

I have changed the pronouns in verses 14 and 15 because they are crucial for our understanding of the passage. God (in v. 14) offers to do *more for Moses* than for the people. The ''rest'' promised to Moses is connected with joy and satisfaction. So the Lord now agreed to personally accompany the people, but *only Moses* is assured of ''rest.'' But that's not what Moses wanted. Thus, in verses 15 and 16 he repeatedly associates himself with the people: ''us . . . with me and with Your people . . . us . . , me and Your people.'' Moses knew what he wanted and he kept asking until it was granted! He wanted the people to share again in a special relationship with God. He wanted them to have ''rest'' too.

After Moses had exercised his freedom to pray, God expressed His freedom to decide. He declared that the people would again enjoy *both* His presence *and* His ''rest.'' God freely chose to show mercy to two and a half million people. Notice that He did not explain this decision by appealing to some Plan formulated in past ages. He said He was acting in response to Moses. That was the freedom of God at work! In an hour of decision a free man asked our free God to take a certain course. God had the sovereign right to say no but He preferred to show mercy.

## Moses Asks for More

Then Moses said, ''Now show me Your glory.''

And the Lord said, ''I will cause all My goodness to pass in front of you, and I will proclaim My name, the

Lord, in your presence. I will have mercy on whom
I will have mercy, and I will have compassion on whom
I will have compassion. But," he said, "you cannot see My face, for no one may see Me and
live" (Ex. 33:18-20).

Bible scholars show little concensus on exactly what Moses was
seeking, but apparently he wanted some direct observation of God.
Literally, he says, "Cause me to see Your glory." Physical sight
seems implied by the Hebrew verb.

In response, God denied him unshielded sight because to see the
Lord's face would kill him (v. 20). This was another decision
combining God's freedom and mercy. But the Lord promised that
Moses would see His glory in terms of His *actions*. The statement
"My goodness" (v. 19) does not refer to a character trait. This
Hebrew word refers to concrete acts of blessing such as abundant
crops and protection from enemies. So Moses would see God's
glory in terms of benevolent actions.

When the Lord said, "I will proclaim My name, the Lord, in
your presence" (v. 19), we need help to understand. To proclaim
His name amounts to giving further explanation of its meaning.
The name "the Lord" means "I AM." But that leaves a basic
question unanswered: "I AM" *what*? The Lord answered that
question some days later when He said, "The Lord . . . the
compassionate and gracious God, slow to anger, abounding in
love and faithfulness, maintaining love to thousands, and forgiving wickedness, rebellion, and sin" (Ex. 34:6-7).

In granting Moses' request to see His glory, the Lord revealed
His character in *relational* terms. But the actions of God toward
Israel provided the means by which to understand these words. As
the Lord spoke of His compassion, He *was showing it* to two and a
half million people who deserved death. While He spoke of forgiveness, He *was forgiving* their great national sin. The character
of God is revealed in the context of events that confirmed His

statement. Moses cannot know God by looking at Him; he must see what the Lord *does*. The same holds true for us.

"I will have mercy on whom I will have mercy, and I will have compassion on whom I will have compassion" (Ex. 33:19b).

These words fully express God's freedom. But I think it is profoundly tragic that many Christians have understood this verse to describe a narrow, exclusive kind of compassion! They make God's words mean, "I'll have compassion on the lucky few who manage to get it. I'll have mercy on a sliver of humanity, and they're fortunate to get *any*." (Usually this is done by understanding Romans 9 as applying to the personal salvation of Christians. But Paul makes it clear in Romans 9:1-5 that God's subject is the people of Israel—*not* the church. Salvation has no part in Romans 9, which pertains to the privileges and favors God extended to Israel and more narrowly to the family of Jacob. No man has a claim on God's favors. So Paul quotes Exodus 33:19 to prove God's freedom in granting favors. [See Rom. 9:15.] By contrast, God has offered salvation to *anyone* who would claim it by faith in Jesus Christ [John 3:16]. However, I am aware that not everyone will agree with me here!)

In the Old Testament context such an understanding looks ridiculous because God is extending His mercy and compassion to the entire undeserving nation of two and a half million people. Rather than dipping out mercy with a thimble, He floods the world with it! The Lord could choose to restrict mercy to a few, but that's not how He uses freedom. His character of love leads Him to offer mercy to all.

Moses' request to see God's glory has significant parallels to Philip's request that Jesus show the Father to the apostles (John 14:8-10). Jesus answered Philip the same way God answered Moses. He called on Philip to draw his conclusions from the miraculous works of God he had seen in his days with Christ. He saw God's glory by means of His *actions*, and so do we.

For a further summary of principles concerning God's freedom, consult the appendix to this chapter where my views on it are summarized.

## Using Our God-Given Freedom

Consider the following ideas and evaluate how they apply to your own life before God.

1. *Accept responsibility for your own decisions and actions.* Some believers don't want freedom because they don't want the responsibility for their choices. They would rather be in a position to blame someone else in case of problems. Others shrink back from freedom because their background has influenced them toward dependency and insecurity. I see this in two main areas:

● Seeking "God's (hidden) will" about a job change, a move, or some other big decision.

I believe every Christian should pray for wisdom from God in making decisions. But to the extent believers are groping for a Plan where God has already decreed the answer, I think it is an utter waste of time. God has established each of us as our own life-managers with delegated freedom to decide and act. He will not abandon us if our choices lack perfection. Searching for God's "perfect will" in such matters absolutely paralyzes some Christians. I think the reason some believers follow this course is expressed in the following: the second main abuse of our God-given freedom.

● Blaming God or others for our problems or poor choices.

To have freedom of choice means we also have some responsibility about the outcome of these choices. Adam freely chose to disobey God and promptly blamed both God and Eve! But blaming *them* was sin because *Adam* had made the decision. It amazes me that some believers smoke for 20 years and then blame God when lung cancer develops. We're free to decide, but we also must live with the consequences.

2. *Accept the limitations of your freedom.* God has designed human beings to need one another as well as to need Him. That's why God directs believers to take an active role in the body of Christ.

☐ I am willing to seek the wisdom of others.

☐ I am willing to receive help from others.

☐ I am willing to allow time for changes to occur in myself and others.

☐ I am willing to accept that some things will happen to me that I would never choose.

3. *Choose to learn and use the principles and commands God has revealed in the Bible.* By wisely using our freedom to learn from God and His Word, we can thus avoid learning things the hard way.

☐ Do you make reasonable use of your opportunities to study God's Word?

☐ Do you evaluate your life and make decisions based on your interaction with revealed truth?

4. *Pray and ask God to get involved.* Our prayers will have greater effect when we recognize *both our freedom and God's.* Don't use "silver platter" prayers. Here are two examples of what I mean by "silver platter" prayers:

● "Make my child become a Christian."

● "Heal my marriage."

If believers pray like that and then *take no personal responsibility to help the situations happen,* they are asking God to hand the answers to them on a silver platter. God expects us to use our freedom to help heal marriages and to help lead children to Christ while praying for His involvement too. However, in some cases we cannot do anything and the freedom God has to act becomes the only feasible possibility.

5. *Acknowledge God's freedom to say no and trust Him to do it lovingly.*

When I was a college senior I fell in love with the woman who later became my wife. Because she was two years behind me in school, I asked the Navy to let me have more time to work on a master's degree. I prayed hard and my request was approved. So I worked longer than really necessary in order to stay near the woman I loved. When I completed the degree, she still lacked one semester, so I asked to work on a doctorate and prayed again. I was turned down flat even though I had top qualifications. I cried. I was crushed, but I didn't need the doctorate. God said no and I'm glad that He loved me enough to deny my prayer.

# A Final Word

God has ultimate freedom. We have been given a degree of that freedom because we are made in His image. I believe the freedom we sense as we live our lives is *real*. That makes us awesome people living eternally significant lives for God.

# Appendix to Chapter 3

## Principles Relating God's Freedom to Ours

1. God is free: He acts and thinks without compulsion or arbitrary restriction.

    a. Mankind cannot compel any of God's actions.

    b. God's actions are *not comprehensively predetermined* or fixed according to some plan of His own making (for exception see principle 3).

2. God has freely chosen to make man in His image, thus granting man *some* freedom.

    a. Mankind is free to choose or reject God (although without divine enablement, all people would reject God).

    b. Believers are free to influence God by their prayers and actions.

    c. Believers are free to choose their actions and thoughts as life-managers under God. God assists or thwarts these actions if He decides to do so.

3. God has freely sworn to carry out *certain* actions which He has explicitly revealed.

    a. God has revealed the fixed elements of His will rather than hiding them. He has no all-inclusive *hidden* plan for events.

    b. Such things as the certainty of a believer's salvation and the certainty of declared events of prophecy are unalterable according to God's free choice.

# 4
# Encountering Life and Death

## God Is Holy

Holiness is one of the most difficult concepts I have ever tried to grasp.

I have heard two kinds of messages on holiness in my experience of church attendance. In the first type the pastor produced in me *a feeling* similar to what some Bible characters must have felt when they encountered God—an "Oh-wow!" form of awe. But I'm a bit emotionally restrained by nature, and any feeling produced in me soon subsided. By the time I hit the church exit, it was gone. At least, in this first type of message I felt better when it was over than I did with the second kind. The second approach consisted of informing me that *all* my problems originated in my failure to fully understand God's holiness. This type didn't help my self-image, but it surely gave my guilt level a tremendous boost.

Grasping God's holiness involves an *attitude* of healthy respect for Him that affects how we live. To help you develop that attitude will be my goal. I hope you will gain something more permanent than a feeling.

# Defining Holiness

The Hebrew word for "holy" means *to be set apart*. For example, the Levites and priests had been set apart as God's exclusive property. They could never return to secular society to become farmers, metal workers, or workers at any other trade. They were holy unto the Lord.

In my desk I have marking pens to write on overhead transparencies. They are set apart for that purpose alone. In a nonreligious sense they are holy.

We can extend this definition to God's holiness. Holiness sums up His entire character because it consists of all those things that set Him apart from us. His power, knowledge, righteousness, and many other factors make Him different from us. He far exceeds us in every area and so holiness summarizes God's godhood (His divine nature or essence).

From sermons I had heard, I began to think of God's holiness primarily as something deadly. First we will consider such a case.

# Encountering Death

After the reign of Solomon, Israel was divided into two nations. More than a century later (in 792 B.C.) Uzziah began to jointly reign over Judah with his father. In his early years, Uzziah feared the Lord and God gave him success (2 Chron. 26:5). "His fame spread far and wide, for he was greatly helped until he became powerful" (2 Chron. 26:15). Uzziah gained a reputation as a builder and as the greatest military commander since King David.

But as the fame of Uzziah increased, his appreciation of God's holiness decreased. We are told that "his *pride* led to his downfall" (2 Chron. 26:16). By studying one particular incident in King Uzziah's life we will open the door to seeing one side of God's holiness. A connection exists between human arrogance and understanding the holiness of God. A proud person does not

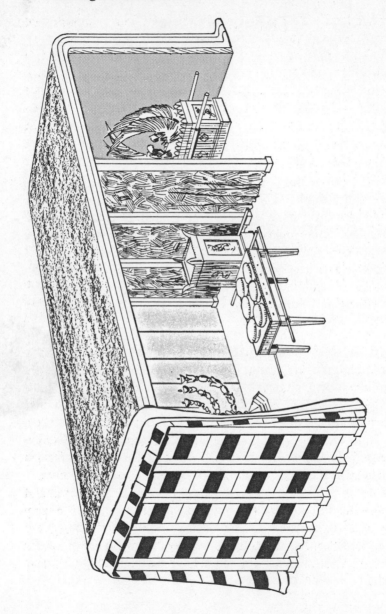

A Sketch of the Temple

understand what sets God apart from man, but a humble and obedient person grasps His holiness.

The Temple of the Lord was divided into two main rooms (see sketch). The innermost room was called the Holy of Holies. It contained the Ark of the Covenant, which was an acacia wood box covered with gold. Two huge figures about 15 feet high overshadowed the ark; they were called cherubim and symbolized the angels serving in God's presence. The ark served as God's throne and from it He ruled His people. The Great King was enthroned in the Holy of Holies.

A curtain divided the inner room from the outer one known as the Most Holy Place. Next to the curtain, the outer room had an incense altar. No person, other than a priest, could enter the Most Holy Place; and only the high priest could pass beyond the curtain into the Holy of Holies on the day of atonement. Before going in, the high priest would take coals from the incense altar, place them in an incense burner (which he held) and begin making clouds of incense to shield him from God's holy presence. This ritual was a matter of life and death.

One fateful day Uzziah entered the temple contemptuously ignoring the absolute prohibition against that. In his hand he held an incense burner (2 Chron. 26:19). He was filling it with coals from the altar when priests burst in to stop him. Uzziah was preparing to go in to the throne room of God! Somehow he had lost sight of God's awesome holiness. But the Lord withheld action while the priests tried to reason with the king. In his pride Uzziah became enraged and I suspect he threatened them with death.

Suddenly the Lord struck the king's forehead with a dreadful skin disease. This supernatural form of judgment wastes the body in a way similar to leprosy. Like Cain, Uzziah had left a holy God out of his reckoning and so received the mark of death upon his head. Like Cain he lived in isolation from his people until his days ended.

Through Uzziah's life we see the harsh side of God's holiness. When an arrogant person holds his fist in God's face, the time will come when the fist rots away. I suspect that you have heard about *this* side of God's holiness—an encounter with death. And I would guess that such incidents make you want to run from His holiness out of fear it may strike you too. That's the way I feel as a sinful man.

But don't shrink back until you see the *other* side of the Lord's holiness, the side He showed to Isaiah.

## Encountering Life

In the year that King Uzziah died, I saw the Lord seated on a throne, high and exalted, and the train of His robe filled the temple. Above Him were seraphs, each with six wings: With two wings they covered their faces, with two they covered their feet, and with two they were flying. And they were calling to one another:

"Holy, holy, holy, is the Lord Almighty; the whole earth is full of His glory."

At the sound of their voices, the doorposts and thresholds shook and the temple was filled with smoke (Isa. 6:1-4).

Uzziah is living out the last miserable year of his life in a house in Jerusalem. Not far from the leprous king, a brilliant young Israelite finds he is in a deadly spot. To his amazement, he finds himself standing precisely where Uzziah was when God struck him. But as Isaiah quivers beside the incense altar, the curtain has been drawn away and he is looking right into the throne room of God!

Isaiah was no more a priest than Uzziah, and, knowing what had happened to the king, he expects to die. In place of the symbolic cherubim he sees a stunning sight. The Hebrew word "seraph" means *burning*; the two angels look like shimmering flames before

God's throne. Instead of the ark, his eyes perceive the Lord's majestic robe covering the floor of the temple. The "smoke" (v. 4) consists of clouds of incense rising from the altar at Isaiah's side. As in the case of the high priest, these clouds shield Isaiah from the face of God. When the seraphs speak, the entire structure trembles. (I think this event caused the titanic earthquake during Uzziah's reign that was remembered for centuries; see Amos 1:1.)

## Will Holiness Bring Death?

"Woe to me!" I cried. "I am ruined! For I am a man of
unclean lips, and I live among a people of unclean lips,
and my eyes have seen the King, the Lord Almighty"
(Isa. 6:5).

Upon seeing the holiness of God, Isaiah understands his own sinfulness. Isaiah sees himself as "ruined," a word used for cities reduced to rubble. He expects to share the fate of Uzziah, but Isaiah has not come to God arrogantly. In fact, he has been summoned by the hand of God. Although Isaiah is a sinful man, he is leading a righteous life before the Lord. And so his experience of God's holiness differs from Uzziah's as day differs from night.

## God's Holiness in Action

Then one of the seraphs flew to me with a live coal in his
hand, which he had taken with tongs from the altar. With
it he touched my mouth and said, "See, this has touched
your lips; your guilt is taken away and your sin atoned
for."
Then I heard the voice of the Lord saying, "Whom
shall I send? And who will go for Us?"
And I said, "Here am I. Send me!" (Isa. 6:6-8)

Here we see how God wants to express His holiness toward mankind. God longs to forgive rather than to judge; to grant opportunities for service rather than death. The Lord works outward from His holy self through the hands of the seraphs to forgive Isaiah's sins. He cleanses Isaiah to make him a man who can serve God and live for Him. That's the other side of God's holiness. God wants to treat us like Isaiah—not like Uzziah.

God not only used His holiness to bring forgiveness, but also as opportunity for spiritual service. Read verse 8 carefully. Many expositors have converted these *questions* into a draft notice. The Lord does *not* tell Isaiah that He has chosen him. He does not violate the freedom of this man (see chap. 3). But He does give Isaiah the chance to freely choose this mission and he gratefully seizes the opportunity. Like Isaiah, believers already enjoy God's forgiveness and so they can use this new status to live for Him.

God's holiness brings us forgiveness and appointment as life-managers. It transforms us into people who want to serve Him as Isaiah did. Holiness can bring death, but God's great desire is for holiness to bring life.

## Our Own Encounter with Holiness

Use the following ideas to evaluate your own response to God's holiness:

1. When you think of God's holiness, how does it affect you?
   - [ ] I sense tremendous distance between us. He's far away, unreachable.
   - [ ] I feel fear because of some current willful sin in my life.
   - [ ] I want to thank Him for my forgiveness and to serve Him in some way.

2. Our freedom and well-being before God can degenerate into pride and arrogance unless we keep in mind the Holy One.

In our home we have a fireplace and I love to get a glowing fire going. As long as I treat that fire with respect, it gives me pleasure. It warms my hands and casts a mellow light into the room. But I don't reach in with my bare hands to move the coals around. I have respect for that fire and no one has to remind me not to touch it. Out of 100 encounters with similar fires I respect them *every time*! That's the kind of attitude we should have about God.

How do you respond to this statement?

- As I look at my life at home and at work, I see evidences of increasing pride.

☐ Yes     ☐ No

In my own life some very pleasing things are happening. I am growing in self-understanding and in professional accomplishments. How easy it would be for my head to swell. My challenge is to remember that success can bring danger of forgetting the Lord's blessings as Uzziah did. Pride can creep in like a glacier—a little each day. What about you?

- Things are generally going well for me and I have *not* lost my thankfulness to God for His grace.

☐ Yes     ☐ No

I'm thankful for: _____

_____

_____

_____

## A Final Word

When I was in ninth grade I quarterbacked the school football team. One day I walked into the gym and saw another boy my age playing keep-away from a group of smaller seventh graders. But as the younger boys came close, the ninth grader would hit them in the face with his clenched fist. His superior strength had gone to his head and he was lording it over everyone.

I don't think he ever saw me until the last second. I wiped him out with a perfect head-on tackle. After I got off of him, I took the ball away, gave it to the younger boys, and told the bully to get lost. (Perhaps it will make you feel better to know I wasn't a Christian in those days. But I think he deserved it anyway!)

Everything was going fine with the boy I tackled until he arrogantly abused his power. God doesn't want to flatten us like He did proud Uzziah, but He will if we insist on it.

The Lord has given us freedom, forgiveness, and opportunity to serve in a context of respect for His holiness. He lovingly desires to treat us like Isaiah who encountered God's holiness and lived.

# 5
# Power for
# a Change

## God Is Powerful

To live we must find and use power. We work to earn money—a key form of power. Education imparts knowledge—a type of power giving us mastery over our world. Social status and personal influence involve another kind of power. Thus, many of our common activities relate to gaining and using power. In fact, the more power we have, the more secure our lives become. That's the way our world works.

As believers, we have access to *the* ultimate power. This planet has only one Superpower and I don't mean America or Russia. The Lord is the only Superpower and to the extent that we learn to utilize His power, we can experience change in our lives.

## A National Crisis

Before the time of Elijah (about 870 B.C.), the nation of Israel had split into two parts. The southern part was known as Judah. The Northern Kingdom was called Israel and Ahab ruled that part. Ahab's father, Omri, had held great power and influence during his lifetime. He arranged for his son Ahab to marry a strong-willed princess of Tyre named Jezebel. She has earned a reputation as one of history's most wicked women. Her father ruled an island city of great wealth and also served as high priest to Baal. So when Jezebel moved in with Ahab, she brought Baal worship with her.

The name Baal means *master* in Hebrew. Like other fertility gods, Baal claimed to give bountiful crops and herds to his worshipers. Ancient stone figures also picture Baal holding a lightning bolt as the god of storms and rain. Baal's supposed rainmaking power gave God a classic chance to show His sense of humor. God sent Elijah to Ahab's palace one day to say, "There will be neither dew nor rain in the next few years except at my word" (1 Kings 17:1). Then Elijah disappeared into hiding. So for three years, Israel, in the realm of Baal, the rain and fertility god, had no rain and disastrous harvests. God was proving that Baal was a zero with no power at all.

Ahab searched everywhere for Elijah, inquiring of every nation about him, but to no avail. Then suddenly Elijah returned and he directed Ahab to assemble all the people at Mount Carmel. This mountain stands on the seacoast about 35 miles south of Tyre, Jezebel's home. Here God's power would challenge Baal.

## The Question

So Ahab sent word throughout all Israel and assembled the prophets on Mount Carmel. Elijah went before the people and said, "How long will you waver between two opinions? If the Lord is God, follow Him; but if Baal is God, follow him."

But the people said nothing (1 Kings 18:20-21).

Seeing how quickly a nation can forget God brings me a feeling of sadness. That applies particularly to a nation founded by God's power. He had freed them from slavery, sustained them during desert years, and conquered a homeland for them. But the memory of His power had faded.

Elijah says, "How long will you waver between two opinions?" The word translated "waver" actually means *to limp along*. Elijah asserts that their lack of commitment to God is crippling them. Later in the passage we will see that this "limping" characterized Baal worship. So Elijah says indirectly that Baal worship cripples Israel. But in spite of his strong words, the people refuse to speak. They kept right on wavering between two opinions in spite of the obvious lack of power in Baal worship.

## The Plan

Then Elijah said to them, "I am the only one of the Lord's prophets left, but Baal has 450 prophets. Get two bulls for us. Let them choose one for themselves, and let them cut it into pieces and put it on the wood but not set fire to it. I will prepare the other bull and put it on the wood but not set fire to it. Then you call on the name of your god, and I will call on the name of the Lord. The god who answers by fire—he is God."

Then all the people said, "What you say is good" (1 Kings 18:22-24).

On the drought-scorched slopes of Mount Carmel stood a beautiful altar to Baal. So his prophets didn't need to build one. Four hundred and fifty finely dressed prophets left the dining table of Jezebel, the real ruler of Israel, to come to this altar.

On the other side of the conflict stands *one* man—Elijah. He has been hiding out for several years, fed by birds and later by a poor widow. I doubt that he had an imposing appearance. And his God has no altar here except some stones scattered through long neglect. What a contrast!

But Elijah confidently proposes the nature of the contest. He even permits the opposition to go first. The people break silence to affirm the plan.

# Super Bowl I

Elijah said to the prophets of Baal, "Choose one of the
bulls and prepare it first, since there are so many of you.
Call on the name of your god, but do not light the fire."
So they took the bull given them and prepared it.

Then they called on the name of Baal from morning
till noon. "O Baal, answer us!" they shouted. But there
was no response; no one answered. And they danced
around the altar they had made (1 Kings 18:25-26).

Now how long do you think it would take for 450 men to prepare
one bull and gather some wood? I would be surprised if it took 15
minutes. In that time they could collect a huge stack of wood for
their god's fiery triumph. After such rapid preparations they had
ample time to pray.

They called on Baal for several hours until midday. Try to
picture the vast quantity of words uttered by so many for so long.
Their chants droned on and on. But what did all these words bring?
The Hebrew text in verse 26 pointedly reads: "No sound. No
answer." Its terse brevity emphasizes the total silence of Baal.

"They danced around the altar" (1 Kings 18:26); but actually
they *limped* around the altar and our study will show us why. Then
Elijah began to have some fun.

At noon Elijah began to taunt them. "Shout louder!" he
said. "Surely he is a god! Perhaps he is deep in thought,
or busy, or traveling. Maybe he is sleeping and must be
awakened." So they shouted louder and slashed themselves with swords and spears, as was their custom, until
their blood flowed. Midday passed, and they continued
their frantic prophesying until the time for the evening
sacrifice. But there was no response, no one answered,
no one paid attention (1 Kings 18:27-29).

I hope you visualize Elijah relaxing in the shade of a tree,
casually chewing a little piece of straw. He needles Baal's

prophets unmercifully. He suggests that Baal may be busy medi-
tating, as gods were thought to do, or sleeping, or traveling.

Then he wonders if Baal is "busy." That translation fails to
show how explicit Elijah's comment really was. I hope what he
really said won't shock you too much. He says Baal may be off
having a bowel movement! If they will just be patient, Baal will
surely return before long. In modern terms Baal is "indisposed."
In this way Elijah mocked their so-called "god."

In response to Baal's silence and Elijah's taunts, the prophets of
Baal cut themselves severely "as was their custom" (1 Kings
18:28). Now you know why *limping* characterized Baal worship.
But their most extreme measures brought no response. The god
named "Master" proved master of nothing. It was necessary for
Baal's prophets to go first and gain every chance at success. Later,
God brought a torrential rain to Israel and if Baal had not been
proven impotent he might have received the credit.

# Final Preparation

Then Elijah said to all the people, "Come here to me."
They came to him, and he repaired the altar of the Lord,
which was in ruins. Elijah took twelve stones, one for
each of the tribes descended from Jacob, to whom the
word of the Lord had come, saying, "Your name shall
be Israel." With the stones he built an altar in the name
of the Lord, and he dug a trench around it large enough
to hold two seahs of seed. He arranged the wood, cut the
bull into pieces and laid it on the wood. Then he said to
them, "Fill four large jars with water and pour it on the
offering and on the wood.

"Do it again," he said, and they did it again.

"Do it a third time," he ordered, and they did it the
third time. The water ran down around the altar and even
filled the trench (1 Kings 18:30-35).

Elijah's preparations look puny in contrast to what his opponents had done. What they did in mere minutes (there were 450 of them) may have taken him as much as an hour. He alone constructed a rough altar, prepared the bull, dug a trench around the altar, and gathered the wood. Then he ordered the sacrifice drenched with water so that no one could claim trickery.

# Holocaust

At the time of sacrifice, the prophet Elijah stepped forward and prayed: "O Lord, God of Abraham, Isaac, and Israel, let it be known today that you are God in Israel, and that I am Your servant and have done all these things at Your command. Answer me, O Lord, answer me, so these people will know that You, O Lord, are God, and that You are turning their hearts back again."

Then the fire of the Lord fell and burned up the sacrifice, the wood, the stones, and the soil, and also licked up the water in the trench.

When all the people saw this, they fell prostrate and cried, "The Lord, He is God! The Lord—He is God!"
(1 Kings 18:36-39)

Baal's prophets had prayed for about eight hours. Elijah prays for about 25 seconds. From the cloudless sky the fire of the Lord falls! Even the stone altar and dust of the ground are consumed.

As I read of this I recalled the first atomic bomb test in New Mexico back in 1945. The bomb had been placed in a steel shack on top of a 100 foot high steel tower. After the explosion the scientists returned to the site, but the steel beams and shack had vanished. They had vaporized in the heat. For 400 yards around the site the sand had fused into green glass.

I see similarities between that test and the power God demonstrated on Mount Carmel that day. Finally, the people cry out that the Lord is God.

# Hindsight

Looking back over this incident, we see a king and people who had no access to ultimate power. They were starving for lack of it. On the other hand, Elijah could summon this power to glorify God.

But when I say that, you will probably say, "Well, sure. He would do that for Elijah." How easily we deify the ordinary men God uses! To read 1 Kings 18 seems similar to getting a glimpse of Superman, but just read the next chapter and see how human Elijah really was. Jezebel threatens his life and he runs away like a scared rabbit. He even asks God to let him die. The victory on Mount Carmel seems to be forgotten.

I believe Elijah was a godly man, but I think you and I can be godly too. A study of the Bible assures each of us an equal share of God's presence. Christ dwells within every believer. But not every believer shares the same degree of God's power. He doesn't just hand that out indiscriminately. Our obedience, prayer life, and commitment to Him all seem to affect our access to God's power. That leads us to the application of this passage to our own lives.

## Access to Power

Use the following ideas to evaluate your access to God's power:

1. Is it possible that divided loyalty or token commitment inhibits my access to God's power?

- Do I visit church now and then for a friend's sake or a spouse's sake? Why do I go to church?
- Do I pray *only* in the face of catastrophe?
- Do I spend time learning what God wants me to do as a believer?
- Do I really belong to Christ or am I just another name on a church roll?
- I believe I am single-minded in my commitment to the Lord.

☐ Yes    ☐ No

2. Are you involved in certain *rituals* designed to unlock God's power? To use ritualism is to treat God like Aladdin's magic lamp. If the lamp is rubbed just right the power comes out. But God's power is not automatic or magic; it's *personal*. Here are some rituals that you may use to stroke the lamp for power.

☐ Do I attend church to stack up "points" with God?

☐ Do I give money or time to put God in my debt?

☐ Do I confess sins, rededicate my life, or go through some other regular procedure to obtain God's forgiveness or power?

3. Each of us can enhance our access to God's *personal power* through:

● Obedience

● Prayer

● Commitment to Christ

James gives us crucial insight here:

The prayer of a *righteous* man is powerful and effective.
*Elijah was a man just like us*. He prayed earnestly that
it would not rain, and it did not rain on the land for three
and a half years. Again he prayed, and the heavens gave
rain, and the earth produced its crops (James 5:16b-18).

Using the Lord's grace and His Word, you can become a righteous person like Elijah.

# A Final Word

In the early 1950's American scientists developed the most awesome energy man has ever found. To test the hydrogen bomb, which even surpasses the atomic bomb's power, one was planted on a coral island in the Pacific. The scientists had heavily armored instruments placed on the island to record the bomb's explosive force. But the power exceeded all estimates, and where the island had once been the ocean now stands 175 feet deep. The instruments and the island both vanished.

The awesome forces slowly coming under man's mastery cannot compare with the power which God has exerted in our world all along. That same power can alter the inner world of our souls bringing growth and change into our lives.

# 6
# The King of Heaven and Earth

## God Is Sovereign

My daily exposure to the news media gives me a sense of anxiety about our world. I feel powerless as if I'm on a train hurtling down the tracks out of control. I'm thankful that God has the authority to take charge of the problem because that gives me hope.

God's authority works hand in hand with His power. Having power means little without the authority to use it. Having authority only matters when power can back it up. God has both.

I have spoken of lacking authority, but another issue also demands attention—abuse of authority. God not only gives hope to those who lack authority, but He can also hold in check those who would abuse authority.

We'll explore these issues in the Book of Daniel which was written by Nebuchadnezzar. Until he properly valued God's ultimate authority, he went through some hard times.

## Babylon's Greatest King

Nebuchadnezzar ruled the Neo-Babylonian empire founded by his father. In his day he surpassed all other kings in both skill and

54

power. He brought Babylon to world supremacy.

As the Book of Daniel begins, Nebuchadnezzar besieges Jerusalem the year after his decisive victory over Egypt, the only other world power. At this point he is the crown prince of Babylon and a capable general. But word arrives of his father's death, so Nebuchadnezzar quickly exacts some treasure and captives and departs for his coronation. Unknown to him, his booty included the greatest national asset Babylon would ever have—a boy named Daniel.

Daniel stands out as a heroic figure in the Bible. Humble, God-fearing, and obedient, he demonstrates how God can stabilize and enrich a man's life in a world that's falling apart. Daniel lacked authority to stop the process as his nation was conquered, and he was taken far away into foreign slavery. But his relationship to the ultimate authority over his world brought order out of chaos. In time, he became the chief advisor to the king:

As Nebuchadnezzar assumed the throne, his other qualities began to show. Picking the cream of each nation, he used these gifted men to increase his power. But as his clout increased, so did his arrogance. Nebuchadnezzar's vast authority went to his head and brought him into conflict with a greater King, the Ruler of heaven and earth.

Nebuchadnezzar tells his own story in the fourth chapter of the Book of Daniel, which is actually the text of a royal decree. He relates a frightening dream in which an enormous tree is cut down by order from a heavenly messenger. But the living stump, bound with a protective metal collar, remains in the grassy field to be drenched with the dew of heaven.

As the heavenly messenger describes what will happen to the stump, he speaks of the stump using *personal pronouns*: "Let *his* mind be changed from that of a man and let *him* be given the mind of an animal, till seven times pass by for *him*" (Dan. 4:16). This will be done "so that the living may know that the Most High is sovereign over the kingdoms of men and gives them to anyone He wishes" (Dan. 4:17).

Nebuchadnezzar sought the meaning of the dream from all the wise men of Babylon, but they could not interpret it. Then he told Daniel the dream and Daniel reacted with intense shock and fear. (Even godly people can properly experience these emotions without detracting from their faith in God.) After regaining composure, Daniel says, "You, O king, are that tree!" (Dan. 4:22) Daniel reveals that Nebuchadnezzar will live like a grazing animal until he acknowledges God's ultimate authority over mankind. Then Nebuchadnezzar's kingdom will be restored.

Daniel's bravery in concluding his session with the king staggers my mind. Such rulers were known to have moody or depressed advisors executed. But Daniel even dares to say, "Renounce your sins by doing what is right. . . . It may be that then your prosperity will continue" (Dan. 4:27). Daniel understands the dynamic freedom of God and wants to see disaster averted. (See Dan. 3.)

## Unchecked Arrogance

All this happened to King Nebuchadnezzar. Twelve months later, as the king was walking on the roof of the royal palace of Babylon, he said, "Is not this the great Babylon I have built as the royal residence, by my mighty power and for the glory of my majesty?" (Dan. 4:28-30)

God granted the king ample time to show evidence of change. But his eyes were too dazzled by his own might. A year after the warning dream, the king strolls on his flat palace roof. The Aramaic verb implies that he did this regularly, perhaps every evening. From this high vantage point the king gazes across the whole city. In every direction stand monuments to his mighty authority. To the south looms the mighty temple of his god Marduk. To the east stretches the city walls, so thick that three chariots could travel side-by-side on top. Under his citadel runs the decorated street down which he had brought so many conquered kings. Nearby to the north he could see the hanging gardens of Babylon which he had built to soothe his wife's homesickness for her lush mountain homeland.

With such vast accomplishments the king was captivated by his own might. That's why the Lord had warned him, but it was to no avail.

## A Sovereign Voice

The words were still on his lips when a voice came from heaven, "This is what is decreed for you, King Nebuchadnezzar: Your royal authority has been taken from you. You will be driven away from people and will live with the wild animals; you will eat grass like cattle. Seven times will pass by for you until you acknowledge that the Most High is sovereign over the kingdoms of men and gives them to anyone He wishes."

Immediately what had been said about Nebuchadnez-zar was fulfilled. He was driven away from people and ate grass like cattle. His body was drenched with the dew of heaven until his hair grew like the feathers of an eagle and his nails like the claws of a bird (Dan. 4:31-33).

God picks the moment when Nebuchadnezzar's pride reaches its peak. "Words fell from heaven" (literal translation of verse 31) at the very instant of the king's words about his own majesty.

The form of insanity supernaturally imposed on the king has also been observed occasionally in modern times. Raymond K. Harrison, an Old Testament scholar, observed such a case in a British mental facility in 1946 (*Introduction to the O.T.*, Eerdmans, pp. 1116-7). It stunned Harrison that the patient had long hair and thickened fingernails described by Daniel. He ate only grass from the hospital lawn. Although such patients act strangely, they retain some sense of self and God just as Nebuchadnezzar did.

To teach the king a lesson, God took him from standing erect on his palace roof and brought him down on his hands and knees to graze like an ox. The metal band protecting the tree stump indicates that Nebuchadnezzar received patient care during his madness. Daniel probably used his powerful position to assure other leaders of the king's eventual recovery. God promised that Nebuchadnezzar could rule again when he admitted the Lord's ultimate authority.

## Turning Point

At the end of that time, I, Nebuchadnezzar, raised my eyes toward heaven, and my sanity was restored. Then I praised the Most High; I honored and glorified Him who lives forever.

His dominion is an eternal dominion; His kingdom endures from generation to generation. All the peoples of the earth are regarded as nothing. He does as He pleases with the powers of heaven and the peoples of the earth. No one can hold back His hand or say to Him: "What have You done?" (Dan. 4:34-35)

Do you realize who is saying these exalted things about God? Not Daniel, but Nebuchadnezzar! This decree circulated throughout his vast empire glorifying the Lord (see Dan. 4:1). Previously the king's vision had remained earthbound; he looked *down* to see his own works. Now he looks *up* to see the real throne over all mankind.

You may find it hard to accept that God inflicted the king with insanity. But consider the great good that it did for him. I'm absolutely convinced that Nebuchadnezzar trusted in the Lord through this experience. His own words imply as much, but another fact makes it conclusive. God refers to only nine men in the Bible by the phrase "My servant." They are all God-fearing Jews like David, Abraham, Moses, and Jesus, except for one— Nebuchadnezzar. Since every other person among the nine believed in the Lord, I'm confident we'll meet this mighty man in heaven.

# Restoration

At the same time that my sanity was restored, my honor and splendor were returned to me for the glory of my kingdom. My advisers and nobles sought me out, and I was restored to my throne and became even greater than before. Now I, Nebuchadnezzar, praise and exalt and glorify the King of heaven, because everything He does is right and all His ways are just. And those who walk in pride He is able to humble (Dan. 4:36-37).

What does it mean to humble oneself before God? Does it mean that we must become miserable beggars renouncing all earthly pleasures? No! God finds no fault in Nebuchadnezzar's wealth and kingly power. God restored him ''even greater than before'' (Dan. 4:36). A man can rightly enjoy great riches and authority when he puts his life under the Lord's ultimate authority.

It's not wrong to have authority, power, freedom, and wealth. The sin comes only in refusing to acknowledge God's sovereign right to rule. Yet I know so many Christians who feel ashamed that God has blessed them. For example, I have heard dozens of spiritually-minded people try to resolve their guilt over having a beautiful house by vowing to use it for the Lord. We *ought* to use our homes for Him, but *not* to atone for the supposed sin of having something nice. A good steward can enjoy his Master's bounty as Nebuchadnezzar's life amply shows.

After returning to power the king develops some new habits. In verse 29 we saw his old custom of strolling around praising himself. A similar Aramaic construction implying *regular* activity occurs when he says, "Now, I, Nebuchadnezzar, praise and exalt and glorify the King of heaven" (Dan. 4:37). From praising himself to exalting God—the king has come a long way.

# The Ultimate Authority Over Us

Use the applicational concepts below to sharpen your own response to God's ultimate authority.

1. If you have an increasing sense of powerlessness and anxiety about the future, how should you respond?

- To put my confidence in the sovereignty of America is not wise.
- To put my confidence primarily in myself will not sustain me.
- I need to recognize and admit my anxiety about the future.
- I need to recognize God as my ultimate basis for security in a deteriorating world. He deserves my confidence!

Daniel lacked the authority to respond to his crumbling world. But his righteous relationship to God, the ultimate authority, brought stability to his life. Daniel remained in power beyond Nebuchadnezzar's death and through the short reigns of four more Babylonian kings. Even when Babylon fell to the Persians, Daniel prospered under them! God's throne is not shaken by the events of this world.

2. Your self-esteem can assume proper dimensions only when your God-esteem is high. With God's approval, Nebuchadnezzar kept a high self-esteem even after he granted the Lord supremacy.

☐ I should not try to elevate God by demeaning myself!

☐ I think I have an esteem for the Lord that fully acknowledges His ultimate authority over my life.

☐ I think I feel free to value myself without ignoring God's authority.

- I can have possessions.
- I can have and use power.
- I can have and use freedom.
- I can have a sense of personal worth and dignity.

I see many Christians struggling with discomfort over the considerable authority God has given each of us. Instead of resisting these blessings, we should *use them* for the Lord!

## A Final Word

Our lives are like a ship crossing the open sea. As the ship travels, the navigator uses his sextant to shoot the stars and fix his own position. We can only understand our authority by taking our position relative to God and His ultimate authority.

In times of uncertainty His authority gives us hope. In times of great success we should remember an ancient Roman custom. As the conquering general returned to Rome with the spoils of war, he received a thunderous welcome from the populace. As he rode through the cheering crowds in a chariot, an assistant would lean forward saying, "Remember, you're only a man."

# 7
# God's Lavish Hand

## God Is Kind

I really enjoy clever books such as *The Peter Principle*. Lawrence J. Peter and Raymond Hull tell how to climb the corporate ladder to success. For example, to rise effectively you must use *pull*, not *push* (Wm. Morrow Publisher, chaps. 4-5). *Push* is the power we can summon from ourselves to succeed by self-effort. It sounds like the American way, but Peter favors *pull*. To use *pull*, you must find a powerful person above you who will consent to become your "patron." The patron then pulls you up through the ranks, if you can figure out how to motivate him!

How fortunate we are to know Christ. Believers don't need to search for an earthly patron to rally to their cause, because in the Lord we have the ultimate Patron. He *already* wants to shower us with kindness. God is *for* me; He is *for* you. In our church we sing a chorus that repeats the words "God is so good." But the punch line comes when we sing "God is so good *to me*."

Some Christians take the Lord's kindness for granted. I recently talked with a lady who had missed church for weeks due to cancer treatments. She didn't realize how much the body of Christ meant to her until she couldn't meet with us. Like her, we all need to enhance our awareness of God's kindness and learn how we can enjoy even more of it.

## The Glory and Wisdom of Solomon

You would have to look long and hard to find anyone who had seen more of God's kindness than Solomon, Israel's third king. Just to mention his name evokes thoughts of wisdom and wealth. Small wonder that his wisdom is proverbial since he wrote most of Proverbs! And his splendor was compared by Christ to the richly colorful flowers of Israel (Matt. 6:29). But we may forget that at one time Solomon had neither wisdom nor wealth. He received these blessings through the kindness of God.

Put yourself in Solomon's place for a moment. How would *you* like to follow David as king? That would threaten most people a lot. David had conquered all the surrounding nations and brought Israel to the height of its power. The people loved him because he had an unassuming way with them. To follow David successfully would take *pull*.

## The Offer of Kindness

Solomon made an alliance with Pharaoh king of Egypt and married his daughter. He brought her to the City of David until he finished building his palace and the temple of the Lord, and the wall around Jerusalem. The people, however, were still sacrificing at the high places, because a temple had not yet been built for the Name of the Lord. Solomon showed his love for the Lord by walking according to the statutes of his father David, except that he offered sacrifices and burned incense on the high places.

The king went to Gibeon to offer sacrifices, for that was the most important high place, and Solomon offered

a thousand burnt offerings on that altar. At Gibeon the
Lord appeared to Solomon during the night in a dream,
and God said, "Ask for whatever you want Me to give
you" (1 Kings 3:1-5).

Because of the influence of David, Pharaoh took the rare step of
forming an alliance with Israel by the marriage of his daughter to
Solomon. Although this practice was followed by most nations,
Egypt often spurned normal diplomacy because of its international
power. With this politically favorable marriage, Solomon began
his reign with a debt to David.

Solomon demonstrated a heart for God at this early point.
Following the model of his father, he kept the commandments of
God. In two matters only does Solomon err. Like David, he
married foreign women. Like the people, he made sacrifices to the
Lord at the high places. Later the high places became malignant
centers of idolatry, but now both king and people ignore God's
edict to worship Him only at Jerusalem (Deut. 12:5). Balancing
these flaws, Solomon's gigantic offering symbolized his great
devotion.

To this young, untried king God extends an unprecedented
chance: "Ask for whatever you want Me to give you" (1 Kings
3:5). That's *pull!* But now Solomon faces a hard decision. In *this*
test David cannot help.

## The Choice

Solomon answered, "You have shown great kindness to
Your servant, my father David, because he was faithful
to You and righteous and upright in heart. You have
continued this great kindness to him and have given him
a son to sit on his throne this very day.

"Now, O Lord my God, You have made Your servant
king in place of my father David. But I am only a little
child and do not know how to carry out my duties. Your

servant is here among the people You have chosen, a
great people, too numerous to count or number. So give
Your servant a discerning heart to govern Your people
and to distinguish between right and wrong. For who is
able to govern this great people of Yours?'' (1 Kings
3:6-9).

Americans generally want to find the "bottom line." So our
minds tend to skip over the first part of Solomon's prayer. But in
verse six we learn why God gave "*great* kindness" to David.
David left us a clue as to how we can experience more of the Lord's
kindness. He became heir to a windfall of generosity by concen-
trating on obedience to God.

This principle will be confirmed in the following passage: *God
gives kindness to all believers, but He gives lavish kindness to
those who please Him.* God's freedom comes into focus here. All
Christians equally enjoy such things as eternal life and forgiveness
for sin. But we each get tailor-made favors according to His
pleasure. So if we live obediently like David, we will enhance the
Lord's generosity toward us.

In making his request Solomon lays great stress on his responsibilities. He humbly calls himself "a little child." This leads him to
ask for what the *New International Version* translates "a discerning heart."

In English the word "heart" has emotional overtones. Thus
evangelicals often contrast "head" belief with "heart" belief.
However, the Israelites ascribed to the heart the functions that *we*
would ascribe to the *mind*. The Hebrew word refers to the seat of
decisions, will, memory, reasoning, and planning (Hans Walter
Wolff, *Anthropology of the O.T.*, Fortress Press, chap. 5). Emotions are not excluded from the "heart," but they are secondary.
So Solomon is seeking *rational* powers as the words "to distinguish between right and wrong" also suggest (1 Kings 3:9).

Consider too what Solomon does *not* ask for. He doesn't seek the "hidden will of God." He doesn't say (as believers so often do), "Tell me what You want me to do next week." He gives no evidence of "seeking God's will" in the way many do today. Instead, Solomon asks for wisdom so that *he* can act as a steward for God. In my opinion, we should shape our requests to be more like his.

## God's Lavish Hand

The Lord was pleased that Solomon had asked for this. So God said to him, "Since you have asked for this and not for long life or wealth for yourself, nor have asked for the death of your enemies but for discernment in administrating justice, I will do what you have asked. I will give you a wise and discerning heart, so that there will never have been anyone like you, nor will there ever be. Moreover, I will give you what you have not asked for—both riches and honor—so that in your lifetime you will have no equal among kings. And if you walk in My ways and obey My statutes and commands as David your father did, I will give you a long life" (1 Kings 3:10-14).

The Lord was emotionally moved by Solomon's choice. As a result He grants him wisdom that surpasses all men of all ages. Verse 12 literally means, "I *have* done what you have asked. I *have* given you a wise and discerning heart." So great is God's power that He speaks of events to come with the same certainty as yesterday's news. I personally see this as the Lord's power to carry out His promises rather than the ability to foresee future events.

Because the Lord is "pleased" with Solomon's desire, His kindness now overflows even more. Not only would Solomon surpass the men of all ages in wisdom, but he would enjoy wealth and glory beyond any ruler of his generation.

Perhaps I'm just a Texas boy who has seen too many old

movies, but what God did for Solomon paints a picture in my
mind: I see an oil derrick on a treeless prairie. Suddenly the ground
rumbles, the derrick top shakes violently and a gigantic column of
oil showers the delirious workers. That's how I envision the
overflowing abundance of God's kindness to Solomon. And I
believe He wants to treat us the same way. As we lead a life that
pleases the Lord, He uncorks a gusher of kindness and loads us
with great benefits.

As God relates to Solomon, we can easily see His freedom in
dispensing favor. But His dynamic interaction with mankind
comes across too. Notice the conditional nature of verse 14: "*If*
you walk in My ways . . . I will give you a long life.*"* God retains
something vital to Solomon, long life, as an opportunity for further
blessing. Sadly, Solomon wasted this chance. He turned from
God's ways later in life and lived a shorter life than David. But in
his early years we see the words of Christ illustrated: "Seek first
His kingdom and His righteousness, and all these things will be
given to you as well" (Matt. 6:33).

## Learning from the Wisdom of Solomon

1. Just as Solomon needed godly wisdom to carry out his
responsibilities, we need it too. Evaluate your own situation:

   ● God has expressed extensive principles of wisdom in
   the Scriptures. How wide is your grasp of these principles?

   | Generally familiar to me | | | Unknown to me | |
   |---|---|---|---|---|
   | 5 | 4 | 3 | 2 | 1 |

   ● Do you *consciously* review principles from God's
   Word as you make choices in daily life?

   ☐ Yes   ☐ No   ☐ Somctimes

   ● Do you ever pray to ask the Lord for a discerning
   mind to guide your life?

   ☐ Yes   ☐ No   ☐ Sometimes

2. God has shown kindness to each of us in different ways. Every believer shares such blessings as forgiveness in Christ and the indwelling presence of the Holy Spirit. But what special kindness has the Lord shown you as an individual?

_____

_____

Have you thanked and praised Him?

☐ Yes          ☐ No

3. Paul tells us in Ephesians 5:1 that we are to "be imitators of God." Beyond any doubt this includes showing kindness to one another (Col. 3:12).

- Would your mate and/or best friend describe you as "kind"?
- Would you describe yourself as "kind"?
- What goal for this week could help you develop and *express* kindness?

## A Final Word

Showing kindness can require sacrifice. My daughter Amy was three when we brought her newborn brother home from the hospital. Amy was delighted to see Scott for the first time. After he had been home about ten minutes, she very quietly slipped off to her room.

Amy was the proud owner of two security blankets, which she called "nah-nah." (The reason she had *two* is because her father is a *very* careful person.) Those blankets meant about as much to Amy's happiness as her parents. As far as she knew, she had the only two "nah-nahs" in the whole world. They were both in captivity in our house.

When Amy came back from her room she brought one precious

blanket and gave it to Scott. "He doesn't have one," she said. I hope you realize that was half the world's supply!

Sometimes being kind can cost us a lot. It cost God a lot to send His Son. But that was just the beginning of what He wants to do for us.

# 8
# The Ultimate Friend

## God Is Self-Disclosing

I may never learn to enjoy my wife expressing anger toward me. But her willingness to disclose how she feels has helped me grow and has dramatically strengthened our marriage.

I'll give you an example. I have a somewhat rigid personality that reacts too quickly to quell playful action and confusion. With three young children in our home, such situations abound! Sometimes our house simply vibrates with activity. I respond by adding control through either rules or discipline. By calming the children's play, I try to protect my easily shattered nerves.

About a year ago my wife expressed her anger to me about my rigidity. She said I had a hard time relaxing and relating to others in playful ways and that affected my adult relationships as well as my parental role. She found this embarrassing and irritating and told me so. That wasn't the most pleasant news I had ever heard, but her loving candor helped me understand myself.

I have personally experienced the constructive power of self-disclosure for about two years, but only recently have I realized why it works. *The reason self-disclosure has such potency to produce change is because it follows the pattern of God's own ways.* God discloses Himself. He has created us in His image, so as we open up with each other we are imitating God.

In fact, the whole biblical account tells how the Lord has revealed Himself to man. He tells us what He is like as well as His feelings, plans, and expectations. God has used self-disclosure to build His relationship to each of us. So it occurred to me that the same technique would naturally build friendship and intimacy on the human level.

But revealing our inner selves also involves risk. My wife took a chance on provoking my anger. I might have rejected her along with her angry feelings. In the same way God took a risk in revealing Himself through Christ. Some trusted in Him, but others flatly rejected Him.

These themes of self-disclosure, intimacy, and risk dominate a story from the life of Abraham. Careful study of it will pay dividends by suggesting how we can develop greater closeness with God and with each other, and thereby produce needed changes in our lives.

## An Unexpected Visit

After moving to Canaan, Abraham had separated from his nephew Lot (Gen. 12—13). Through Abraham's graciousness in giving him first choice, Lot had picked the fertile land of the Jordan Valley for his home. Prior to God's judgment on Sodom and Gomorrah, this land was unsurpassed (Gen. 13:10). Lot pitched his tents near Sodom, already known as a wicked place, while Abraham dwelt in the mountains overlooking the Jordan Valley. Many important years passed before God promised Abraham a son through his wife Sarah (Gen. 17). For a man of 100 years and a woman of 90 years, that was no small matter. But Abraham believed it.

One hot day Abraham was surprised to find three "men" near

his tent (Gen. 18:2). He didn't know their identity (Heb. 13:2), but with Sarah's help he showed them customary hospitality. Sarah remained hidden from their sight, as was also proper, so she never imagined who had come.

# Disclosing Identity

Then the Lord said, "I will surely return to you about this time next year, and Sarah your wife will have a son."

Now Sarah was listening at the entrance of the tent, which was behind him. Abraham and Sarah were already old and well advanced in years, and Sarah was past the age of childbearing. So Sarah laughed to herself as she thought, "After I am worn out and my master is old, will I now have this pleasure?" (Gen. 18:10-12)

What a shock this must have been to Abraham! The speaker could only be the Lord, who had first given him this great news some days before (Gen. 17:21). In my opinion, the Lord Jesus Christ spoke to Abraham that day. (Such an encounter could explain Jesus' remarks to the Jews in John 8:56.) For the first time since Eden, God revealed Himself to a man in bodily form. What a stunning disclosure!

The revelation of His identity provides the first of four disclosures made to Abraham during this visit. However, Sarah thinks only of the promise as she overhears these remarks. She does not grasp who has spoken.

The *New International Version* translates it thus: "Sarah laughed to herself" (Gen. 18:12). Literally the Hebrew word means *in her inward parts*. If you had stood beside Sarah that day, you wouldn't have heard a sound. Since the "inward parts" refer to a realm unseen by man, Sarah's response amounted to hidden unbelief. This leads to God's second disclosure to Abraham on that eventful day.

# Unbelief and Anger

Then the Lord said to Abraham, "Why did Sarah laugh and say 'Will I really have a child, now that I am old?' Is anything too hard for the Lord? I will return to you at the appointed time next year and Sarah will have a son."

Sarah was afraid, so she lied and said, "I did not laugh."

But He said, "Yes, you did laugh" (Gen. 18:13-15).

The Hebrew text has several emphatic words which probably imply the Lord's anger over Sarah's unbelief. So the Lord reveals His emotional state to Abraham as a vital part of this marvelous picture.

Sarah's inner reaction to the Lord's words now gets full exposure as her unspoken thoughts are revealed to Abraham: "Will I *really* have a child . . . ?" The Hebrew word translated "really" is used when a person considers an event contrary to possibility. Sarah's doubting question actually amounts to a statement: "I will certainly *not* have a child." This skeptical word "really" is first found in the mouth of Satan as he said to Eve, "Did God *really* say, 'You must not eat from any tree in the garden'?" (Gen. 3:1) By using this word, the Lord captures the essence of Sarah's rejecting attitude.

So God's second disclosure to Abraham uncovered Sarah's unbelief and His own anger. Abraham must have felt sadness and anger toward his wife's behavior. Her sin disrupted their good relationship.

Then Sarah depicts her own inner state, but the picture she paints is a lie. (Before judging her too quickly, we may need to ask how often *we* mask our feelings from others.) The Lord directly confronts her with the truth.

I believe Sarah would have received forgiveness and understanding if she had humbly sought it. But false self-disclosure effectively blocks intimacy in any relationship.

## Revelation Restricted
When the men got up to leave, they looked down toward Sodom, and Abraham walked along with them to see them on their way. Then the Lord said, "Shall I hide from Abraham what I am about to do? Abraham will surely become a great and powerful nation, and all nations on earth will be blessed through him" (Gen. 18:16-18).

This change of scene flows directly out of Sarah's faithless response. God discloses Himself and lovingly risks rejection, but unbelief sometimes causes him to curtail revelation. Jesus followed this pattern as He shifted from open teaching to parables in reaction to unbelief (Matt. 13:12-13). Only His disciples learned everything (Matt. 13:11). The Lord certainly intended to reveal His plans about Sodom to Abraham, but He would say no more in the presence of Sarah. So the two angels, the Lord, and Abraham begin the descent into the Jordan Valley toward Sodom.

For a reflection within the mind of God, look at Genesis 18:17-19. The same verb occurs here that represents Sarah's thought life in verse 12. The Lord has a reason for unmasking His plans to Abraham. H. C. Leupold gives a masterful translation of Genesis 18:19 in which the Lord states His purpose:

> For I acknowledge him to be *My intimate friend* to the end that he may enjoin upon his children and his household after him to keep the way of the Lord to do what is just and right, in order that the Lord may bring upon Abraham that which He promised him (*Exposition of Genesis*, Vol. 1, Baker Book House, p. 544).

God looked on Abraham as His "intimate friend"! In fact, Abraham is called "My friend" (see Isa. 41:8) by Him in several places. It was to further build this relationship that the Lord revealed His intentions to Abraham. Recent psychological research also suggests that sharing secret information promotes intimacy between friends (Hillix, Harari, and Mohr, "Secrets," *Psychology Today*, Sept. '79, pp. 71-76). But beyond deepening the relationship, God wanted Abraham to lead his family into righteousness so that He could bless them even more. Based upon these inner desires, the Lord makes the third disclosure to Abraham.

## Disclosing Judgment

Then the Lord said, "The outcry against Sodom and Gomorrah is so great and their sin so grievous that I will go down and see if what they have done is as bad as the outcry that has reached Me. If not, I will know" (Gen. 18:20-21).

You may feel tension here between God's knowledge of all that is happening and His investigation of this sin. But remember that God is disclosing Himself and His ways. The "Judge of all the earth" (Gen. 18:25) is demonstrating to Abraham, Lot, and others that His judgments are not arbitrary but according to fact. He is *visibly* checking out the charges for *their* benefit, not His own.

## Doubt and Concern

The men turned away and went toward Sodom, but Abraham remained standing before the Lord. Then Abraham approached Him and said: "Will You sweep away the righteous with the wicked? What if there are 50 righteous people in the city? Will you really sweep it away and not spare the place for the sake of 50 righteous people in it? Far be it from You to do such a thing—to kill the righteous with the wicked, treating the righteous and the wicked alike. Far be it from You! Will not the Judge of all the earth do right?" (Gen. 18:22-25)

One of the 18 instances in which the ancient scribes of Israel changed the Hebrew text to save face for God is found in verse 22

(Gleason A. Archer, *A Survey of O.T. Intro.*, 2nd ed., Moody Press, p. 61). The verse originally read, "the Lord remained standing before Abraham." The scribes apparently felt this demeaned God, but actually it shows His great love for Abraham. The Lord knows Abraham is seething with concern for Lot. Abraham has long known the wickedness of Sodom and he realizes that judgment will inevitably fall. So the Lord pauses to encourage self-disclosure *by Abraham*. He stands silently to show His willingness to listen to His friend. Abraham picks up the hint immediately and approaches the Lord.

With great feeling Abraham discloses his doubts and concerns. His candor involved risk as he didn't know how the Lord would react to his emotions and requests. I imagine he felt fear as he recalled God's anger with Sarah. But his inner state bears little resemblance to her's. She reacted with unbelief in the face of concrete details while Abraham reveals honest doubts from *a believing heart*. He seeks enough facts to calm his concerns. Abraham is struggling to reconcile God's righteousness and justice with His obvious intent to destroy Sodom. Thinking of Lot's family, Abraham believes there are some righteous people living there. By revealing his inner turmoil to the Lord, Abraham sets the stage for the fourth disclosure from God.

## Disclosing Mercy and Justice

The Lord said, "If I find 50 righteous people in the city of Sodom, I will spare the whole place for their sake" (Gen. 18:26).

God reveals to His friend that He will respond to the righteous with mercy and justice. He keeps on confirming this as Abraham risks pleading for Sodom even if only 10 righteous people dwell there (Gen. 18:32). Abraham was taking a chance in the lengthy interaction. Although Abraham's final number was still too high, the Lord demonstrated His character by getting the few righteous out before sending destruction. By his courageous self-disclosure, Abraham learned about the extent of God's mercy and His willingness to dynamically interact.

## Learning to Be God's Friend

Use the following tools to analyze your own relationships.

1. Through the model God gave him, Abraham developed an honest, self-disclosing relationship with Him. Evaluate your own level of openness with the Lord in communicating your doubts, feelings, and needs:

☐ I relate to Him like Sarah; I disclose little to Him.

☐ I relate to Him like Abraham, with considerable candor.

☐ Sometimes I communicate openly, and other times not.

Perhaps one issue you need to resolve is this:

☐ Do I really want to have an intimate friendship with God? He wants it with you! (See John 15:15.)

2. How we respond to God's self-disclosures will affect how much further insight we receive from Him through the Holy Spirit. He shows great patience, but He also responds more favorably to us as we trust what He says.

● Do you see a correlation in your own life between honestly seeking to follow His ways and experiencing more insight into His Word?

☐ Yes    ☐ No

## Learning to Be a Friend Like God

The degree to which we practice self-disclosure will determine the number and quality of our friendships. Sadly, even husbands and wives may not be close friends. Current research on families indicates that healthy families have:

1. Openness in interpersonal communication.

2. Recognition and acceptance of individual differences.

3. Intimacy in the husband/wife relationship.

In his remarkable book on families, Jerry M. Lewis tells of a 46-year-old engineer who had been happily married for 22 years (*How's Your Family?* Brunner/Mazel, p. 83). But as the years passed, the man realized that something was lacking. Working late, he began talking to a secretary. For the first time he experienced an intimate friendship which eventually led to sexual unfaithfulness. But the basis of this adultery was not sex; it was intimacy that he had never experienced with his wife. We may get by without self-disclosure for many years, but sooner or later we pay a price. Being made in God's image, we are self-disclosing people and vitally needing ways to experience it.

## Evaluate Your Own Style of Relating

● I have at least one intimate friendship.

☐ Yes      ☐ No

After conducting in-depth research on 40 men, Daniel Levinson of Yale expressed the opinion that, "close friendship with a man or a woman is rarely experienced by American men" (*The Seasons of a Man's Life*, Knopf, p. 335). If as a man you marked "yes" above, then you are a rare and fortunate person.

● My marriage and/or best relationship is characterized by considerable self-disclosure.

☐ Yes      ☐ No

## A Final Word

For over 30 years I had no intimate friends; I was both popular and lonely. But self-disclosure has changed all that for me.

As I said earlier, my wife and I have used this process to reduce my rigidity. We have also discussed my lack of playfulness with our best friends who have also helped me—at times more than I wanted! One night we were all playing a game on our living room floor. While I wasn't looking, my wife and friends exchanged a silent signal. Before I knew what had happened, they jumped on me and all tickled me until I thought I would die. I hadn't been that far out of control in years. My rigid personality was appalled at such unseemly behavior! They took the risk of making me angry because they loved me and wanted to help me enjoy life more. I smile every time I remember the incident.

God has modeled self-disclosure so that we can *all* enjoy life more. He wants us to become more than just His servants. He wants us to become His intimate friends.

# 9
# The Unique Center of Life

## God Is Unique

What would you do if you had only one week to live? My own first reaction to that question was that I would have one last ski trip with Kay and the kids. That made me laugh at myself for being such a ski nut.

I'm sure I would spend my final week with my family and closest friends. We would look at what my life had meant—what I had lived for. Looking at both the past and the future, I would want to say things to help them on their way. To say something of lasting value might prove difficult, but I would try.

I hope that I never have to face that task. The Bible reveals how Moses responded to such a test. His words are recorded in the Book of Deuteronomy.

## The Brink of Victory and Death

Moses may have had as little as one week to live as he stood before the people on the plains of Moab (Deut. 1:1-5). To the west about seven miles stood Jericho on the other side of the Jordan River. Beyond the city the Israelites could see the mountainous backbone of Canaan. After 40 years of wandering, the people paused on the brink of their inheritance. But their entry was Moses' exit. Death loomed over him and he knew it (Deut. 31:2, 14).

Moses had risked his life for the Israelites many times. For 40 years he had loved them and eventually led them to this place. What would he stress in his final days with them? The answer brings us to the core of the Old Testament—to what Jesus called the greatest commandment. Similar to Moses, Jesus stressed these same ideas in His teachings during the last days before *His* death on the cross.

## The Unique Center

Hear, O Israel: The Lord our God, the Lord is one. Love the Lord your God with all your heart and with all your soul and with all your strength (Deut. 6:4-5).

Should we think of verse 4 as an exercise in mathematics? No, its main thrust lies elsewhere. It answered the gnawing uncertainty which plagued all people living under polytheism. Literally dozens of gods demanded their worship (over 80 in Egypt alone). This promoted fatalism because it was commonly believed that even one neglected angry god could inflict misery on a person. As Israel prepared to enter another land of many gods, the people needed a refresher course.

In view of this background, I prefer this translation of verse four: "The Lord our God, the Lord is the *unique* one," (author's translation). Moses stresses the one-and-*only* specialness of God, who rules over every area of life. To Him *alone* they could pray for such diverse things as fertile crops, victory in war, and forgiveness for sins. That's what made Him so unique and incomparable. Certainly God is numerically one, but to place our attention on that fact is to miss the main point.

With this interpretation verse 5 makes better sense to me as well. It does not call on me to strain and grit my teeth to love God

harder. Rather, He becomes the unique center of my *entire life*.
The progression "heart . . . soul . . . strength" probably means
"the inner person . . . the whole person . . . the actions of the
person" based on the typical usage of the Hebrew words. The Lord
deserves to become the focal point of my whole life because He is
Lord of *all*. That's a far cry from the narrow, specialized gods of
the Egyptian world.

## Response to Uniqueness—Part 1

These commandments that I give you today are to be
upon your hearts. Impress them on your children. Talk
about them when you sit at home and when you walk
along the road, when you lie down and when you get up.
Tie them as symbols on your hands and bind them on
your foreheads. Write them on the doorframes of your
houses and on your gates (Deut. 6:6-9).

After declaring God's specialness and the chief implication of
this fact, Moses commands the people to saturate themselves and
their children with the knowledge God has revealed especially to
him.

The Lord's commands should be "*impressed* on your children"
(v. 7). The Hebrew verb *impress* first meant to sharpen a knife or
spear by repeated strokes. It later came to mean "to say something
again and again." Educators have long recognized that repetition
plays a crucial role in learning. Moses tells us in the remainder of
the verse that every life setting will be affected by God's commands. These different contexts give believers the challenge to
integrate faith into everyday life.

The Pharisees of Jesus' day showed rare skill in keeping the
letter of God's Law while missing its whole point. In response to
Moses' message in verse eight, they strapped small boxes contain-
ing Scriptures to their foreheads and arms. These boxes were
called phylacteries. Unfortunately God's Word never seemed to

penetrate their minds, and Jesus condemned their acts of externalism. Knowledge is a means, not an end. Memorizing Scripture or having several Bibles in the home cannot replace real living for God, but knowledge does help us get started·

Before treating the second half of our response to God's uniqueness, Moses deals with three dangers which threaten the Lord's special role in our lives.

# The Danger of Abundance

When the Lord your God brings you into the land He swore to your fathers, to Abraham, Isaac, and Jacob, to give you—a land with large, flourishing cities you did not build, houses filled with all kinds of good things you did not provide, wells you did not dig, and vineyards and olive groves you did not plant—then when you eat and are satisfied, be careful that you do not forget the Lord, who brought you out of Egypt, out of the land of slavery (Deut. 6:10-12).

It had been easy to focus on God in the years of wandering. By day the pillar of cloud shielded Israel from the burning sun. At night the pillar of fire warned off marauders. The people had no food or water except what the Lord gave. Manna was wisely designed to spoil after the first day so that each family had to face their daily dependence on God. Even their shoes and clothes were prevented from wearing out over the years!

Soon they would seize Canaanite cities, houses, wells, and vineyards to meet their physical needs. But such plenty held the seeds of a terrible harvest; they would be tempted to forget the Unique One.

In America we enjoy an unusual degree of our world's wealth. It protects us from many terrors that others know. We are especially threatened by an abundance that dulls our sense of need for our unique God. But affluence isn't our only worry.

## The Danger of Substitution

Fear the Lord your God, serve Him only and take your oaths in His name. Do not follow other gods, the gods of the peoples around you; for the Lord your God, who is among you, is a jealous God and His anger will burn against you, and He will destroy you from the face of the land (Deut. 6:13-15).

Religious cults lurk in every American city, but for most of us they do not threaten to take God's place. We are more inclined to allow other things to crowd the Lord out by subtle degrees. One person might become absorbed in work while another thinks only of his children and a third drives himself to reach a life goal. Rather than idols we face the danger of good things usurping the Center of our lives. Israel, on the other hand, would soon face actual idolatry.

Moses uses the word order of verse 13 to push home his point: "*The Lord your God* is the one you must fear. *Him only* you must serve. *In His name* you must take your oaths." My literal translation shows how Moses put the Lord at the head of every clause for emphasis.

The danger of apostasy leads directly to the idea of God's "jealousy" (v. 15). This word refers to an *uncompromising intensity* that the Lord would show in defending His holiness and His covenant relationship with Israel. They had knowingly entered into a binding relationship with God. He became their God and they became His people. To respect the depth of this arrangement, the Bible frequently used the analogy of marriage. Thus, idolatry is called adultery and produces feelings of jealousy because of the third party involved.

I'm sure Moses experienced emotional pain while saying these things. He had felt the brunt of the Lord's anger at Mt. Sinai when the people worshiped the golden calf. So Moses did not consider these dangers merely theoretical because he had the scars to prove them. He loved the people and deeply cared for their future. This time they would be tempted without him.

# The Danger of Rebellion

Do not test the Lord your God as you did at Massah (Deut. 6:16).

One painful memory often prompts another. For Moses to recall Massah was to remember both personal and national tragedy (see Num. 20:1-13).

The parents of those now with Moses had long ago rebelled against him at Massah because they saw no source of water. Now their children were "testing" God at Massah. To sin against God again added insult to injury. The whole Exodus generation had already destroyed their chance to enter Canaan; their children very nearly did the same.

To "test" someone means to push him to his limit. God's patience and long-suffering nature were being stretched to the breaking point. Small children often illustrate such testing behavior in relation to a parent's authority. One day my wife was waxing our kitchen floor and having a running battle with our two-year-old son Scott. Scott was told repeatedly to stay off the wax, but he would stand at the door and hold his foot in the air right over the forbidden area. He was blatantly testing his mother! That may work with mothers, but not with God.

To resolve the crisis, God told Moses to take his staff (a reminder of past miracles) and call forth water from a rock there, *using words alone*. That's when Moses lost the whole ball game. In direct disobedience to the Lord's clear instructions, he struck the rock with his rod instead of using words. In view of Moses' intimate relationship with God, this act took on tragic dimensions. Because he had dishonored the Lord before the nation, he forfeited the right to enter Canaan.

Now, as Moses faces imminent death, he does not spare himself from painful memories if it will help his people appreciate the uniqueness of God.

## Response to Uniqueness—Part 2

Be sure to keep the commands of the Lord your God and the stipulations and decrees He has given you. Do what is right and good in the Lord's sight, so that it may go well with you and you may go in and take over the good land that the Lord promised on oath to your forefathers (Deut. 6:17-18).

Based on his own failure to obey the Lord's express command at Massah, Moses returns to his previous positive emphasis. Earlier he had stressed the importance of knowledge. Now he urges godly behavior and promises resultant blessing.

The Lord will continue to interact with the people in a dynamic way. Note the conditional nature of verse 18. Moses and the first generation had lost their inheritance in Canaan. The fate of those standing on Jordan's banks would depend on their response to the uniqueness of God.

## Applying the "Specialness" of God

Use these concepts to refine your own response to the Lord:

1. Sometimes people think of God's power and rule as extending *only* over spiritual matters. Like the local gods of the Old Testament world, we may think of the Lord as seldom setting foot outside the church. But part of His uniqueness consists in His supremacy over *all of life*. With all candor, which of the following areas of your life do you see as relevant to God?

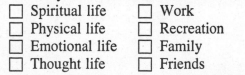

All of us would say God cares about our spiritual lives, but in our heart of hearts we may not allow Him to connect with us in "secular" matters. Francis Schaeffer expresses it this way: Jesus is Lord over the whole spectrum of life. God cares about our sexual relationship to our mate, what kind of friends we have, and how our incomes are spent. That's His uniqueness.

2. Recent studies reveal that most men attach great significance to only a few elements of their lives. I suspect that women do the same thing. Try to rank the following areas in the order of importance they have in your life using numbers 1—7. Consider not only how much time you currently spend, but what you would pick if forced to make a choice.

_____ Occupation

_____ Family

_____ Friends

_____ Achieving status or a personal dream

_____ Continuing your relationship with God

_____ Money or possessions (getting or using)

_____ Other (sports, hobby, etc.)

● Are the areas of your most intense focus causing you to "forget the Lord"?

It may prove difficult to know whether God actually ranks number one in your life. But if He isn't a leading contender for that spot, then you may have fallen prey to a danger that threatens the unique place God deserves to have in your life.

3. One of the hardest things for Christians to accept is their own personal value in God's sight. This view has arisen from an overemphasis on mankind's sinfulness, and the mistaken idea that we must become "nothing" in order for Christ to use us. We are trained to fear the slightest hint of "pride."

But each of us has been created in the image of our unique God (Gen. 1:26-27). That makes you a special person, with unique identity and value before God. You can feel good about what God has created without sinning through pride or arrogance.

How do you feel about signing your name in the following sentence? _____ *is a uniquely valuable person made in the image of God.* If you cannot sign that blank with good feelings, then you are suffering from a common evangelical hangover (mankind's nothingness). To counteract the overemphasis on this idea, I recommend for your reading an excellent book on the subject: *You are Someone Special* by Bruce Narramore (Zondervan).

I hope you can sense how strongly I feel about this point. I have always known that every human being was unique, one-of-a-kind. At last I know why; God made us each special to represent His own uniqueness. If you don't know yourself very well, take the time to learn exactly who you are. You're that valuable!

# A Final Word

Some years ago Albert Einstein told an assistant that he only wanted to find out one thing. He wanted to know the thoughts of God; then everything else would be a simple matter of details. Einstein had an appreciation for how unique God really is, but his appreciation was only theoretical. It never became part of his daily life.

How is it with you? Is the uniqueness of God a nice idea or a living reality at the center of your life? You may have many years of life ahead. Why not live them with the *unique* Son of God at the center?

# 10
# Caring When It Hurts

## God Cares

Having others who care about us can spell the difference between life and death. Researchers have found this particularly true in high stress situations. For example, combat units were studied to learn why men suffered mental breakdowns in battle. This hardly ever occurred when the group had a buddy system or some other strong sense of caring for each other (James J. Lynch, *The Broken Heart*, Basic Books, pp. 100-101).

Also people suffering in Nazi concentration camps could withstand extreme conditions if they felt strong support from other prisoners. But if a man was suddenly transferred away from those who cared, he would commonly lose hope, fall into despair, and die. So under high stress, a sense of others caring can sustain the will to live and stay in the fight.

But you are probably not living under such extreme conditions, so what value does caring give you? In more "normal" levels of stress, caring from others and from God makes a vital difference too. It can give you the will to go on another day—the will to achieve something for God.

Several things can block caring and prevent its healing work. Cultural pressures form one barrier. I encountered this in a recent experience in a large grocery store. As I was leaving, a small, crying boy came running between the checkout lines. He had lost his mother and was feeling panic. I knelt down to his level and held my arms out to him. I was quite willing to help him find his mother, but someone else wasn't quite so sure—the head cashier. She was watching and trying to decide if I was some creep who would carry the child out the door and get the store sued for millions. Even in the simple act of helping a child I had come under suspicion. Caring for others often has a price tag of one kind or another. (To set your mind at rest, we found the child's mother.)

Another obstacle to caring is that the person who needs it may not be very attractive to us. He may not look like our kind of folk. The little boy in the store looked very much like my own son. He was about three years old, had blond hair, and carried a little truck in his hand. But what if he had been a grubby little kid with a runny nose? Would I have wanted to hold him quite so readily?

Some people who need care hold those who would care at arm's length, and that's the third barrier. Ironically, people with two very different styles of behavior can act this way. The very good and the very bad don't seem to want caring from others. The former don't think they ever need it and the latter feel unworthy of getting it. Super saints and super sinners often resist concern shown by others.

Jesus met each of these walls to caring in His ministry. How He responded to them will show us what God is like and define a path for us to follow.

## Jesus the Wall-Breaker

We see Christ repeatedly risking His reputation to care for others in Luke 7. First He agrees to go to the home of a Gentile to heal his servant. It wasn't socially acceptable for godly Jews to mix with

Gentile "dogs." To make matters worse, the Gentile was a Roman and part of the occupation army.

Next, Luke tells of Christ's shocking behavior at Nain. Encountering a funeral procession, Jesus was moved with compassion by a widow who had lost her only son. Defying the traditional ritual of the uncleanness of death, the Lord actually touched the coffin before summoning the boy back to life.

Jesus cared for others even when it hurt. He knew He would be condemned by His religious enemies. They made sure that the price of caring was high.

## The Face of Opposition

"For John the Baptist came neither eating bread nor drinking wine, and you say, 'He has a demon.' The Son of Man came eating and drinking, and you say, 'Here is a glutton and a drunkard, a friend of tax collectors and "sinners." ' But wisdom is proved right by all her children." (Luke 7:33-35)

As Jesus speaks to a crowd in Galilee, He reacts to the criticism that He has received. He does this by contrasting the reception the people (especially the religious establishment) had given to Him and John the Baptist. John led an ascetic life in the wilderness, calling people out from a wicked generation. They wrote him off as demonic. On the other hand, Jesus mixed freely with every level of society, but Jesus' style of caring found no more acceptance than John's. Because He was willing to eat with those who needed salvation, they called Him a "glutton and a drunkard."

To make Christ even less popular, the religious leaders called Him a "friend of tax collectors and sinners." Good people should certainly shun such a man.

But Jesus says that both He and John are "children of wisdom" (i.e., those living wisely). Their different ways of caring would ultimately be vindicated.

## Dinner with the Very Good and Bad

Now one of the Pharisees invited Jesus to have dinner with him, so He went to the Pharisee's house and re-clined at the table. When a woman who had lived a sinful life in that town learned that Jesus was eating at the Pharisee's house, she brought an alabaster jar of per-fume, and as she stood behind Him at His feet weeping, she began to wet His feet with her tears. Then she wiped them with her hair, kissed them, and poured perfume on them.

When the Pharisee who had invited Him saw this, he said to himself, "If this Man were a prophet, He would know who is touching Him and what kind of woman she is—that she is a sinner" (Luke 7:36-39).

The Pharisees were men who had taken certain *vows* about ceremonial purity and tithing. (Pharisaism bears some similarity to a fraternity. To have contact with something unclean or to fail to pay religious tithes amounted to breaking their vows.) Some Pharisees had a theological education, but most did not. Men who had theological training were called scribes and some of these were leading Pharisees.

Luke tells us in verse 36 that Jesus "reclined at the table." This should be explained. In the Pharisee's house a banquet room had a low table surrounded by low couches. Imagine the table as the hub of a bicycle wheel and the couches as spokes. The dinner guests would rest one elbow on the table and their feet would extend away toward the walls.

The Pharisee extends common hospitality to an itinerant rabbi and His disciples by inviting them to dinner. In exchange he expects a lesson in religious law. Such behavior was customary.

Everything went fine until the arrival of an unexpected guest. I'm sure the Pharisee was stunned when he saw her enter because she was a well-known "sinner." I believe she was a *prostitute* for four reasons. Women did not customarily go out alone in public, but she did. And never would a respectable woman go out unveiled—a sign of loose morals. But Simon the Pharisee recognized this woman right away, so she had no veil. She also wore her hair down, another common sign for prostitutes. Finally, it was considered unseemly for a woman to touch a stranger as she was touching Jesus. You can imagine how agitated Simon the Pharisee must have felt to have her drop in at dinner.

Luke's verb tenses inform us that the woman *kept on* wiping the tears with her hair, kissing His feet, and pouring perfume on them. For any of this to happen was bad enough; for it to go on and on was unthinkable!

Simon thought to himself, "If this Man were a prophet, He would know who is touching Him and what kind of woman she is—that she is a sinner" (Luke 7:39). To help you feel the way the Pharisee did about this woman, try to imagine the following: It is late at night and you get up from bed and wander into your kitchen in the darkness. You think about turning on the light, but you really don't want to wake up that much. Suddenly a roach crawls across your foot! Yuk! That's the way Simon felt about this unclean woman and her conduct with Jesus. I'm sorry to subject you to that feeling, but it's a close emotional experience in our own culture.

But Simon's thoughts reveal more: "*If* this Man were a prophet . . ." (Luke 7:39). The Greek language has a special way of indicating whether he felt this assumption was true, which he didn't. It could be translated, "This Man can't be a prophet or He would know who is touching Him, which He doesn't." So Simon rejected the possibility that Jesus came from God because He had contact with sinners.

## A Lesson in Caring

Jesus answered him, "Simon, I have something to tell you."

"Tell me, Teacher," he said.

"Two men owed money to a certain moneylender. One owed him 500 denarii, and the other 50. Neither of them had the money to pay him back, so he canceled the debts of both. Now which of them will love him more?"

Simon replied, "I suppose the one who had the bigger debt canceled."

"You have judged correctly," Jesus said (Luke 7:40-43).

Jesus had been invited to give a lesson in religious law, so He begins. He will use His lesson along with the actions of the sinful woman to teach the uncaring Pharisee of his own spiritual need. That was Jesus' way of caring for Simon.

The details of the lesson need not detain us because Jesus uses it simply to get Simon's assent to an idea. The rabbis frequently used debts of money as symbols of man's debt of sin before God. Jesus wants Simon to agree that a *great expression of gratitude gives evidence of a great debt of canceled sin.* Simon acknowledges that this is true. After Simon takes the bait, Jesus begins to reel him in.

Then He turned toward the woman and said to Simon, "Do you see this woman? I came into your house. You did not give Me any water for My feet, but she wet My feet with her tears and wiped them with her hair. You did not give Me a kiss, but this woman, from the time I entered, has not stopped kissing My feet. You did not put oil on My head, but she has poured perfume on My feet. Therefore, I tell you, her many sins have been forgiven—for she loved much. But he who has been forgiven little loves little" (Luke 7:44-47).

It may amuse you to consider why Jesus asks Simon, "Do you see this woman?" Simon hasn't been able to think of anything else since she arrived, but he probably avoided looking at her. As part of His lesson the Lord draws his attention to her.

You may think Jesus is rebuking Simon about the water, the kiss, and the oil, but He isn't. Courtesy did not require any of those things, so Simon did not fail as a host. He acted correctly and politely, nothing more. But by comparison the sinful woman has shown every mark of voluntary gratitude that the culture allows and that in the face of social rejection. By any standard "she loved much." So to make His first key point, Jesus contrasts her behavior with Simon's. The point is expressed in verse 47, "Therefore, I tell you, her many sins have been forgiven as is known by the fact that she loved much" (author's translation). Simon can scarcely deny this because he previously agreed to it in principle.

Jesus' second key point hits closer to home with Simon. "He who has been forgiven little loves little." Jesus could have added that the one who doesn't show any love at all hasn't been forgiven anything! That was Simon's case as demonstrated by his minimal hospitality. Jesus truly cared for him by revealing his need for forgiveness.

## Caring When It Hurts

Then Jesus said to her, "Your sins are forgiven."

The other guests began to say among themselves, "Who is this who even forgives sins?"

Jesus said to the woman, "Your faith has saved you; go in peace" (Luke 7:48-50).

Having contrasted the different behavior of Simon and the prostitute, Jesus indirectly contrasts their spiritual conditions. As far as the Pharisees were concerned, she had long ago passed beyond hope. Her sins had mounted until she was lost beyond redemption. So when Jesus declared, "Your sins have been forgiven" (literal trans.), the guests came unglued. Only God could authoritatively forgive sins, so they considered Jesus' remarks blasphemy. But just as they failed to understand her gratitude, they failed to grasp His authority.

Jesus began taking increasingly greater risks to highlight their need for salvation. We see Him caring for the very bad and the very good even when it could only bring Him further rejection. Can you imagine what shameful distortions of gossip would come from this prostitute kissing His feet?

Jesus shows us that God cares even when it hurts. And we are to imitate His ways (Eph. 5:1).

# Time for Self-Evaluation

Use these applicational concepts to measure your own ways of caring:

1. How popular would Jesus be today? By contemporary standards His relational ways seem abrasive. Many of us tailor our actions so as to keep everyone happy and pleased with us. We avoid disagreement or conflict with others like the plague. Jesus didn't act like that! He didn't retreat at the first sign of anger or resistance. He cared about others enough to cut through to the heart of their true needs.

Enormous cultural barriers may inhibit us from "speaking the truth in love" (Eph. 4:15) to our mate, children, or friends. Many of us have been raised to believe it's wrong to upset people or let them feel anger. By our social rules Jesus would be classified rude, but He didn't let that stop Him from caring. If we live as salt and light in this world, we will care enough to confront all those whom we love.

How about you?

- Would I dare invite Jesus to dinner?

  ☐ Yes    ☐ No

- What is stopping me from relating to others with candor about my needs and theirs? Could the peaceful atmosphere between us simply reveal a lack of caring?

  ☐ Yes    ☐ No

2. Families have a general composite attitude toward others outside their families. Some families think of others as generally bad and not to be trusted. These inward families confine intimate relationships to those within their homes. Other families have a more positive attitude toward outsiders and seek intimate relationships with them.

- In which type of family would Simon be more comfortable:

  ☐ Inward    ☐ Outward

- In which type of family would Jesus fit the best?

  ☐ Inward    ☐ Outward

- Which style of family is most like my own?

  ☐ Inward    ☐ Outward

3. Along with the potential for great rewards, caring about others exposes us to possible pain and rejection. Think of your most vital relationship (your mate or best friend). To follow Christ in caring even when it hurts, what is the most caring thing you can do today to strengthen that relationship?

4. Do you identify with the notoriously sinful woman? As you feel remorse and sorrow for sin, can you also accept Christ's total forgiveness and tender caring for you?

## A Final Word

Pauline Kael was raised in San Francisco near the wharf area known as the Embarcadero. She grew up in hard times, the years of the Great Depression. As she accompanied her father, she saw the long bread lines of men out of work.

Some of those men would knock at the back door of Pauline's home to beg for food. Her mother fed them and as a result got angry criticism from the neighbors. They asked Pauline's mother what she would do when hundreds more came. She said, "I'll feed them till the food runs out" (Studs Terkel, *Hard Times*, Pantheon Books, p. 35).

Jesus was like that. He cared for others even when it cost His life on the cross. He's not calling on us to give our lives, but He wants us to care about others even when it hurts.

# 11
# The
# Accepter

## God Accepts

Most of us would do just about anything to be accepted. In fact, acceptance holds a strong position among life's themes. Nations shape their policies, companies set their product prices, and people trim their profiles all for acceptance.

Each of us wants to fit in. Some of us want to fit in at the local country club. Or at a sewing club. Or in a new neighborhood. Even churches develop reputations for their readiness to integrate new people. Becoming part of a group gives us a boost, because it meets our need for belonging.

But if *gaining* acceptance means so much, then *showing* acceptance becomes critical too. If so many of us need it, then many others must know how to give it or pain will result. Many hurting people provide evidence that the supply of acceptance doesn't meet the demand. Abraham Lincoln knew this. Once he was asked how he would treat the people of the Confederacy as they returned to the Union after the Civil War. He said that he would treat them as though they had never been away.

How do we achieve acceptance in our most vital relationships?

The answer to this question will uncover the basic structure of our relationships. In this chapter we will pay particular attention to our relationship to God and His acceptant nature. Then our family and friendship ties will move under the spotlight.

## Jesus Defends Himself

In chapter 10 we saw the steady barrage of criticism that Jesus faced in caring about others. At one point in His ministry, the Lord defended His tolerant ways by telling three parables. He did this in response to the charges of the scribes and Pharisees. Like a dripping faucet they kept saying, "This Man welcomes sinners and eats with them" (Luke 15:2). The entire 15th chapter of Luke deals with this attack and Christ's answer. In the three parables Jesus identifies with the acceptant attitude of the Father toward repentant sinners. By comparison the scribes and Pharisees rejected "sinners" whether repentant or not.

In the first parable a man loses one of his hundred sheep. When he finds it, he rejoices just as God does when one sinner repents and comes to Him.

Next, Jesus tells of a woman who lost one of ten silver coins. She seeks that lost coin diligently until she finds it. By analogy, God unrelentingly searches for repentant sinners. The climax comes, however, when Jesus tells about a father who lost one of two sons. The stories progress from a hundred sheep to ten coins to two sons. A lost sheep has value, and a lost coin even more so, but who can count the worth of a lost son? The final parable dominates the three by its length and character development. Most people know it as the Parable of the Prodigal Son, but the central figure is actually the accepting father.

## Tragic Loss

Jesus continued: "There was a man who had two sons. The younger one said to his father, 'Father, give me my share of the estate.' So he divided his property between them.

"Not long after that, the younger son got together all he had, set off for a distant country and there squandered his wealth in wild living" (Luke 15:11-13).

In crafting this story, Jesus intentionally gives the man *two* sons. Each son represents one of two factions. The older son portrays the intolerant Pharisees while the younger son depicts the sinners trying to return to God. The father shows us God's attitude toward each group. By designing the story carefully, Jesus answers the criticisms of the Pharisees and gives comfort to the repentant sinners simultaneously. In other words, the parable flows directly out of the historical context in which these conflicting interests gathered around Christ.

Knowing the provisions of Jewish law, the father did not have to grant the younger son's request, but he did. The complex legal situation would probably yield to the younger son 20-25 percent of his father's estate with the remainder going to the older son. *But as long as the father lived he had the right to income from both parts of the estate.* Both shares comprised the father's retirement money and he could draw funds from either son's part as he wished. Only when the father died would the sons' legal responsibility to him end.

Before continuing with the story, we need insight into the relational perspective. Both sons are alienated from the father. For a young son to leave his father in this way proves his discomfort by the standards of that time. The older son stays home, but as the story develops the gulf between him and the father emerges. The father will overcome one son's alienation, but not the other's. To understand the parable we must bear in mind that such stories teach one main point. The story leaves many questions unanswered because they don't affect the central issue. We are not told how the two sons (i.e., the Pharisees and sinners) became alienated from the father (God). It will do us no good to wonder how the father would have responded to an appeal for more money to replace what was lost. The parable does not reveal God's basis for accepting sinful people.

After converting his inheritance into cash, the wayward son heads for a distant country. This remote goal symbolizes how far the less religious people of Israel had drifted from their spiritual moorings. It didn't take the young man long to blow the whole thing. That demonstrates how unready he was to leave his father's home in the first place.

## Out of the Frying Pan, Into the Fire

After he had spent everything, there was a severe famine in that whole country, and he began to be in need. So he went and hired himself out to a citizen of that country, who sent him to his fields to feed pigs. He longed to fill his stomach with the pods that the pigs were eating, but no one gave him anything (Luke 15:14-16).

When the wealth has vanished, a famine reduces the boy to hunger and desperation. He hires himself out to a Gentile to care for pigs. Jesus describes the plight of the younger son in increasingly serious terms. Every step he takes brings him farther down. First, he leaves his home prematurely. Then he joins himself to a pagan, which would cause a Jew to shudder. Worse still, he takes a job forbidden by the Law. Finally, if anything is worse than feeding pigs, it's wanting to eat their food. To Jewish minds, the boy hit rock bottom.

To translate the younger son's state into our culture, consider this analogy. Imagine that a teenage son runs away from home with a substantial share of the family money. He begins to associate with some bad people in a distant city. Then he gets a job selling illegal drugs. Finally he becomes addicted to drugs himself. This analogy will give you a feel for what this boy had done.

## A Change of Heart

"When he came to his senses, he said, 'How many of my father's hired men have food to spare, and here I am starving to death! I will set out and go back to my father and say to him: Father, I have sinned against heaven and against you. I am no longer worthy to be called your son; make me like one of your hired men.' So he got up and went to his father" (Luke 15:17-20a).

Give this boy credit. He had behaved like a fool, but when he crashed he faced the facts squarely. He knew that he had sinned against both heaven and his father. He had sinned against heaven by breaking the fifth commandment as then understood. It says, "Honor your father and your mother" (Ex. 20:12), which isn't done by blowing their retirement money! Naturally, that also involved a sin against his father. Hear carefully his key words, "I am no longer *worthy*." This statement sharply differs from what the older son will say. Drawing attention to his years of slavish labor, the older son will argue that *he is worthy*. The younger son has reached the right conclusion; by his behavior he deserves nothing. After rehearsing his confession, he starts the long trek back home.

## Acceptance Plus!

"But while he was still a long way off, his father saw him and was filled with compassion for him; he ran to his son, threw his arms around him, and kissed him.

"The son said to him, 'Father, I have sinned against heaven and against you. I am no longer worthy to be called your son.'

"But the father said to his servants, 'Quick! Bring the best robe and put it on him. Put a ring on his finger and sandals on his feet. Bring the fattened calf and kill it. Let's have a feast and celebrate. For this son of mine was

dead and is alive again; he was lost and is found.' So
they began to celebrate'' (Luke 15:20b-24).

The father's welcome to the wayward son never fails to move
me deeply. It symbolizes God's attitude of acceptance toward a
sinner who seeks a relationship to Him. Remember that the father
*does not know what the son is going to say.* What the father *does*
know is that he wants to heal the alienation of his son. Casting
propriety to the wind, the old man runs to meet his son in a
complete reversal of custom in a father-dominated society. The
father cares nothing about what certain rigid people (like the
Pharisees) will think of his actions.

The *New International Version* translates verse 20, ''He *threw*
his arms around him and kissed him.'' The first verb implies
intense action similar to football players grasping for a fumble. He
*kisses* the son fervently as the same Greek verb demonstrates in
other instances (Acts 20:37; Luke 7:38, 45).

Only now does the confession come. Here we see no hint of
arrogance or claim of rights even after the warmest greeting from
his father. He wants relationship to his father on any terms, even as
a hired slave. He knows better than to expect that he can return to
his former status.

But the young man soon gets the shock of his life. The father
restores him to a higher level of privilege and power than he has
ever had. He gets the best robe, the seal-ring of authority, and
sandals from the hands of those beneath his new status. This
illustrates how God's riches overflow toward those who turn to
Him with nothing worthy to show. God raises them to the highest
place without regard for their works *because the relationship is
what He really wants*.

Deep down, doesn't it bother you that the boy gets all this?
Inside aren't you thinking, ''This kid doesn't deserve it''? But
your discomfort reveals that you are judging the younger son based
on his works. The fact that it bothers you also shows that you don't

approve of the structure the father wanted for this relationship. The father accepts the son *with absolutely no regard for his actions*. He accepts the boy because of who he is, not based on what he has done. That makes the whole difference in this parable.

I think this radical structure is what God wants in life's most vital relationships. For example, husbands and wives should *not* relate to each other on the basis of what they do for each other. Their fundamental acceptance of each other must take priority over what they ''deserve'' on the basis of actions. Consider the alternative way: a husband only loves his wife when she acts right. When she doesn't, he stops loving her because she no longer deserves it. Or a parent only loves a child when he performs properly by making good grades and ''being good.'' I believe that God wants us to show acceptance in these vital relationships *no matter what*.

I don't think God intended that acceptance be preferred to performance in every human relationship. In *business* relationships, performance generally matters above anything else. When you hire someone to fix your car, the only acceptable outcome is that it works. If you contract for termite extermination, the only thing that satisfies the structure of the relationship is that the termites die. Such relationships do rest on a performance basis.

I hope you realize that I *like* good performance or good works as well as anyone. I'm simply saying that life's most vital relationships must rest on another foundation. God doesn't dump us when we sin and that ought to tell us something.

## A Heart Centered on Performance

''Meanwhile, the older son was in the field. When he came near the house, he heard music and dancing. So he called one of the servants and asked him what was going on. 'Your brother has come,' he replied, 'and your father has killed the fattened calf because he has him back safe and sound.'

"The older brother became angry and refused to go
in. So his father went out and pleaded with him. But he
answered his father, 'Look! All these years I've been
slaving for you and never disobeyed your orders. Yet
you never gave me even a young goat so I could celebrate with my friends. But when this son of yours
who has squandered your property with prostitutes
comes home, you kill the fattened calf for him!' " (Luke
15:25-30)

Not everyone joined in the celebration. The older son reacts
with a plentiful supply of anger, stubbornness, jealousy, and
bitterness. Why? Careful analysis of his words tells all. In verse 29
he says, "All these years I've been slaving for you," and the
present tense of the Greek verb implies that he still is. He speaks
with the dirt of the fields on him. The older son reveals that his
vital relationships are based on a *performance standard of acceptance*. He is alienated from his father and he's trying to *earn* his
father's acceptance.

When the older son speaks of never disobeying his father's
orders, Jesus is using him to illustrate the long list of rules which
the Pharisees said men must meet to be acceptable to God. The
Pharisees carried the same structure into human relationships.
They only related to those who behaved by their rules. All others
were dirty "sinners."

Consider further the far-reaching significance of a performance
standard in our own culture. No wonder unborn children can be
aborted in our society; they don't do anything to earn their way.
Euthanasia of old people makes sense in a world keyed to performance. When relationships are based on something other than a
person's worth as a human being, then we must make sure we
never get sick or have emotional problems because we may become expendable.

Not only does the older son judge himself by actions alone, but he does the same in evaluating his father and brother. His father failed to give him a young goat and his brother acted foolishly. So he has rejected them both.

This dismal scene lasted for some time. The verb forms in verse 28 disclose that the father kept pleading with him, but the older son remained adamant.

## The Final Question

" 'My son,' the father said, 'you are always with me, and everything I have is yours. But we have to celebrate and be glad, because this brother of yours was dead and is alive again; he was lost and is found' " (Luke 15:31-32).

If you have heard many messages on this parable, you may be wondering if the central theme really is *acceptance*. But notice where the parable stops. It leaves us hanging! Jesus doesn't tell us whether the older boy will ever come in. How perfect.

Jesus leaves the ball right in the Pharisees' lap. Will they come in and share the Father's joy over the return of the wayward sinners? It all depends on whether they can share His accepting heart and cast away their rule-oriented approach to people.

Jesus is identifying Himself with the accepting father (God). He is trying to restore the alienated sinners and tax collectors who are returning to God from far away. He values them not for their performance but because God values the relationship above everything else.

## Accepting and Being Accepted

We can't change the Pharisees, but we can focus on our own needs. Use these applicational ideas to guide you.

1. Do you identify with. . .
   ☐ The younger son—seeking acceptance from others, feeling unworthy of it

☐ The older son—accepting self and others only on a performance basis

☐ The father—accepting others without extreme demands

If you are a perfectionist, you should identify with the older son to some extent. You probably don't accept yourself when you fail to meet your own high performance standards. I know that struggle well!

2. Right now I feel . . .

Acceptable  1  2  3  4  5  Unacceptable
. . . to my mate or best friend.

Before looking at item three, remember that the younger son did not get the robe and ring until he revealed his repentant heart. God isn't saying He accepts anyone and everyone *on any basis*. He has some minimal requirements which are not grounded on performance.

3. What minimum standards do you demand from others before accepting them as friends? The higher and thicker your acceptance walls become, the fewer your close friends will be. As a result loneliness may put extreme pressure on you someday. The Pharisees had high standards and few friends.

4. Which of the following are trying to *earn* acceptance with you?

☐ Your mate          ☐ Your children
☐ Your best friend      (quite common)
                    ☐ Your brothers, sisters

Are they doing this to please you? Someday they may quit playing the game! They may want a friend who will love them for what they *are* rather than for what they can *do*.

5. Of the following, who are *you* trying to earn acceptance with?

☐ Your mate
☐ Your best friend

☐ Your boss
☐ Your children
☐ Your parents, brothers, sisters
☐ God
☐ Yourself

Do you only feel acceptable to God when you have done your Bible study or witnessed to someone lately? These are wonderful things, but they are *not* necessary to gain His acceptance. We should live for God because He has already accepted us.

6. How do you go about getting acceptance?

- Sex
- Money (making enough to please someone)
- Decisions (letting the other person make them)
- Freedom (giving it up)
- Restricted emotional expression (never show anger or disagree)
- Role playing (super wife, super husband, super Christian)

Why are you *earning* acceptance? Is that the only alternative? Discussing the whole issue might spare you years of needless performing.

# A Final Word

Americans are consuming tranquilizers by the tons because they are trying to perform at levels unprecedented in human history. The resultant stress is enormous.

I should know. The "S" on my own Superman shirt is getting a little faded. Lately I haven't felt like I could leap tall buildings at a single bound—or even two bounds. For days I felt terrible because I wasn't *doing enough* for my wife and best friends to keep earning their acceptance. I felt like a worthless failure.

You know what I found out? When it had become obvious that I was failing to *earn* their acceptance, I learned something amazing. They loved me anyway! Not for what I could *do* for them, but for myself. That realization transformed my life. Now I'm living to enhance these relationships and not trying to earn them. That's a whole different ball game!

I learned how God relates to us from my wife and friends. He longs to throw His arms around us even though we don't deserve it.

# 12
# The Exit Maker

## God Saves

The sun was setting on a day of triumph. With dimly lit snow-capped peaks stretching for a hundred miles, the view was incredible. But the four men who could see the falling shadows paid scant attention to the triumph or the view. In their expert judgment the curtains were closing on their lives and they would never see another nightfall. Darkness halted further descent. The west face of Mount Everest had been conquered, but the price of victory would be death.

They huddled close to one another at 28,000 feet with no tents, sleeping bags, or oxygen to resist the frigid night. The temperature plunged to $-20°F$—low enough to kill them on all but the rarest night. But by a stroke of luck the wind stopped all night and that saved their lives. At dawn they stumbled into the highest camp on frostbitten feet to the amazement and joy of those waiting. Great victory had given way to certain death and then to miraculous deliverance.

At certain points in life we need luck in order to come out all right, but sometimes that's not enough to get us through. God has given us great resources to meet life's trials. Being made in His image, we have great mental abilities and freedom to serve as life-managers for Him. But like a tidal wave swamping a small boat, life can overwhelm our resources at times. In such moments only one thing can snatch us from the hungry jaws of disaster; the Lord must deliver us. How will He react when we get in over our heads?

## From Victory into Disaster

How the Lord responds to our crises emerges clearly in His handling of the Exodus from Egypt. Pharaoh spurned God from the very beginning: "Who is the Lord that I should obey Him and let Israel go?" (Ex. 5:2) But through 10 mighty miracles the Lord forced Pharaoh's reluctant agreement to release Israel. He even influenced the Egyptians to give great wealth to the fleeing slaves (Ex. 12:35-36). It was like walking out of prison and having the warden hand over his wallet.

With sudden freedom and wealth the people marched triumphantly out of Egypt. Moses says they went with "a high hand" (Ex. 14:8, author's trans.) which communicates a mood of defiance and self-confidence. This high feeling would be shattered by day's end.

The Lord took Israel on a surprise detour as He directed them to leave the main road to Canaan and move south to the shores of the Red Sea. He was stoking the furnace for a hot crisis.

Learning of the sudden move south, Pharaoh assumed the people were confused and lost (Ex. 14:3). By seizing this opportunity he could avert the disastrous economic loss of the slave race. So Pharaoh and an elite group of officers set out in 600 chariots with a cavalry escort to recapture the people now trapped between sea and sand. If some of the slaves died being taken, that wouldn't matter. Pharaoh thought they were too numerous anyway.

During World War II in North Africa the allies fought many

tank battles in the desert against Germany. An attacking force could be seen for miles due to huge dust clouds stirred up by the movement. As the shadows of evening signaled the end of a great day, Israel's camp felt the sudden chill of fear as a great cloud of dust loomed in the west. As surely as the darkness, the Egyptian mobile force would soon fall upon them. Great victory would yield to death and slavery.

## Onrushing Disaster

As Pharaoh approached, the Israelites looked up, and there were the Egyptians, marching after them. They were terrified and cried out to the Lord. They said to Moses, ''Was it because there were no graves in Egypt that you brought us to the desert to die? What have you done to us by bringing us out of Egypt? Didn't we say to you in Egypt, 'Leave us alone; let us serve the Egyptians'? It would have been better for us to serve the Egyptians than to die in the desert!'' (Ex. 14:10-12)

The first sight of danger sufficed to break the fragile confidence the people had in Moses and in the Lord. And in view of their military status the danger seemed even more acute. Although Israel had 600,000 men, they had no weapons or training. How could they resist the world's best troops?

I find it easy to feel critical toward the Israelites from the quiet security of my office. But when I think of crises I have faced, I recall how the strength of the threats and the presence of my weaknesses captured my attention. Once I was floating in a narrow river channel after ending a water ski run. As my friends turned the boat to get me, I looked up to see another boat coming straight at me. My life vest prevented either swimming or diving deep so I had to watch and listen while the spinning propeller passed just three feet away! The Israelites must have felt as helpless and desperate as I did in the river.

Moses answered the people, "Do not be afraid. Stand
firm and you will see the deliverance the Lord will bring
you today. The Egyptians you see today you will never
see again. The Lord will fight for you; you need only to
be still" (Ex. 14:13-14).

To his credit Moses kept his head longer than the people. He
calmed them with assurances that the Lord would deliver them. I
think he did so on the basis of past experiences with God rather
than knowledge of what God would do. Day after day Moses had
risked his life by approaching Pharaoh and the Lord had delivered
him from danger every time. So it seems reasonable that his
confidence in the Lord would be great.

I believe Moses unwittingly uttered a prophecy when he said,
"The Egyptians you see today you will never see again." He
didn't know an exit, but he knew an exit-maker. For Moses to
speak from his experience with God rather than from knowing His
plans solves a problem in verse 15.

## The Unfolding Plan

Then the Lord said to Moses, "Why are you crying out
to Me? Tell the Israelites to move on. Raise your staff
and stretch out your hand over the sea to divide the water
so that the Israelites can go through the sea on dry
ground. I will harden the hearts of the Egyptians so that
they will go in after them. And I will gain glory through
Pharaoh and all his army, through his chariots and his
horsemen. The Egyptians will know that I am the Lord
when I gain glory through Pharaoh, his chariots and his
horsemen" (Ex. 14:15-18).

Verse 15 has troubled commentators for centuries because God
apparently rebukes Moses and we aren't directly told why. But I
think the problem can be simply resolved by making two reasonable assumptions. First, after Moses had assured Israel of rescue,

absolutely nothing happened! Time passed and the Egyptians advanced unchecked. Second, I assume that even Moses' nerve broke when the danger came so near. As a result he too "cried out" to the Lord in the same bitter way the people had before (v. 10). The same Hebrew verb is used in both cases.

God was imposing a trial so great that even the most spiritual man lost hope. *By setting deliverance in a context of complete hopelessness, God demonstrates that His action is not based on our faith but on His character.* He delivers us because that's His nature.

The Lord reveals the exit to Moses in verse 16; they would escape through the sea. But God has several purposes in mind. He tells Moses to divide the waters by raising his staff. Moses and his staff became the visible symbols of God's power at work. The events inspired trust in *both* the Lord and Moses.

> Then the angel of God, who had been traveling in front of Israel's army, withdrew and went behind them. The pillar of cloud also moved from in front and stood behind them, coming between the armies of Egypt and Israel. Throughout the night the cloud brought darkness to the one side and light to the other side; so neither went near the other all night long (Ex. 14:19-20).

At the last instant the Lord moves His forces to meet the attack. The towering column of cloud shifts quickly between the two "armies." To call Israel an "army" smacks of divine humor because the only available weapon was God's mighty hand. That would soon prove sufficient to dismantle the well-oiled Egyptian military machine.

As night fell, the darkness over the Egyptians had supernatural origin. On their side of the pillar of cloud came a gloom so deep that they could neither see nor move. This "darkness" is the same as that of the ninth plague (Ex. 10:21-23) where the same Hebrew word occurs. And just as the Israelites enjoyed light during that plague, so now the same light helps them flee in the dead of night.

While the troops of Pharaoh were enshrouded in blackness, the two million fugitives crossed the sea between two foreboding walls of water. Such an experience undoubtedly frightened them, which leads to another aspect of God's using crises. Consider that He could have worked the Exodus differently. Pharaoh's forces could have been destroyed before they even reached the city limits. Or Israel could have been shifted to the far shore by sheer miracle. Why did the Lord execute the Exodus as He did?

Only by letting the people experience the danger and fear could God cause them to understand His deliverance. Without feeling trapped in deadly peril, some might have attributed their escape to luck, skill, or their own faith. But God put them into a trial where luck and skill were useless and every person's faith had failed. In such a case God's willingness to save *because it's His nature* becomes crystal clear. I think He treats us the same way at times. He permits overwhelming trials so we can feel the power of His deliverance, even when our faith has collapsed.

God's way of teaching differs from ours. We teach *concepts* such as "God delivers us from disaster." As a result the learners hold the idea in their minds, but time leads to memory loss. The idea weakens as the clock turns. The Lord often teaches by means of *a process of events*. Both the mind and the emotions then become involved in driving God's ways deep into our hearts.

## Stunning Reversal

Then Moses stretched out his hand over the sea, and all that night the Lord drove the sea back with a strong east wind and turned it into dry land. The waters were divided, and the Israelites went through the sea on dry ground, with a wall of water on their right and on their left.

The Egyptians pursued them, and all Pharaoh's

horses and chariots and horsemen followed them into the sea. In the morning watch the Lord looked down from the pillar of fire and cloud at the Egyptian army and threw it into confusion. He made the wheels of their chariots swerve so that they had difficulty driving. And the Egyptians said, "Let's get away from the Israelites! The Lord is fighting for them against Egypt" (Ex. 14:21-25).

As the people began to reach the far shore, I think the pillar of cloud moved behind them into the deep canyon of water. The Egyptians pursued as closely as they could and the predawn hours found them in the middle of a trap. Now the hunter became the hunted. Chariot wheels bogged and broke. Crying out with voices of panic, the Egyptians made a run for it. They shouted God's personal name, "the Lord," which their Pharaoh had demeaned months before. But the tide had shifted against them—for the last time.

## Death and Deliverance

Then the Lord said to Moses, "Stretch out your hand over the sea so that the waters may flow back over the Egyptians and their chariots and horsemen." Moses stretched out his hand over the sea, and at daybreak the sea went back to its place. The Egyptians were fleeing toward it, and the Lord swept them into the sea. The water flowed back and covered the chariots and horsemen—the entire army of Pharaoh that had followed the Israelites into the sea. Not one of them survived.

But the Israelites went through the sea on dry ground, with a wall of water on their right and on their left. That day the Lord saved Israel from the hands of the Egyptians, and Israel saw the Egyptians lying dead on the shore. And when the Israelites saw the great power the

Lord displayed against the Egyptians, the people feared
the Lord and put their trust in Him and in Moses His
servant (Ex. 14:26-31).

Does deliverance really matter? Ask the Egyptians! In *their*
moment of crisis they cry out, but there is no one to rescue them.
Their god Pharaoh stands powerless on the western shore as they
perish. He cannot save them.

But on the eastern shore stands the pillar of cloud, the symbol of
Israel's Deliverer. Not one person has been lost in the crossing.

The Hebrew verbs for "see" and "fear" are almost identical.
Moses uses both in verse 31 to highlight the connection between
what Israel saw and its emotional impact. They saw God's might to
save and so they feared Him. Notice too that the Lord has firmly
established Moses. You can be sure that when Moses stretched out
his hand to talk, people listened!

## Our Need for Deliverance

Many of us will find it hard to identify with Israel because our
crises have not been so severe. What then can this aspect of the
Lord's personality have to do with us?

To show how central deliverance is to God and to us, let's look
at what the angel told Joseph before the birth of Christ: "You are to
give Him the name Jesus, because He will save His people from
their sins" (Matt. 1:21). The name of God's Son, Jesus, means
"The Lord saves." The name Jesus is adapted from the Hebrew
word for deliverance that occurs twice in Exodus 14.

Use the following paragraphs to sharpen your own appreciation
for what God has saved you from and what He will continue to do
for you.

1. In saving us from our sins, God has delivered believers from
*certain spiritual death*. We were trapped between our sinfulness
and the wrath of God against sin. The cost to God to make an exit
for us was enormous—the Son of God had to die in our place.

Interact with these statements about your salvation:
- I better understand today the desperate spiritual plight I was in when I trusted Christ.

☐ Yes          ☐ No

Do you really understand now that all was spiritually lost?

When I trusted Christ as a college senior, I was doing just fine. I knew I had done some wrong things and could see that God would be upset about it. But I had lived a good life and felt my conduct would certainly minimize my guilt before God. Taking security in my works, I had lost perspective on the seriousness of my spiritual condition. In fact, I was spiritually dead and headed for well-deserved eternal punishment. God rescued me from certain spiritual death. Do you now see your salvation in that light?

- I feel grateful to God for making my salvation possible.

A lot          A little
5      4      3      2      1

On the day after the Exodus Israel was bursting with gratitude to the Lord. But the feeling faded as time passed. The same holds true for me. I can't work up the depth of emotion I once felt and I don't think God expects me to. But I can express a quieter form of gratitude by continuing to thank God for my salvation.

Do you thank God often?

- If God had not made salvation possible, my life would have been very different in ways like:

_____

_____

_____

_____

That's a hard question! My wife and I each became Christians at about the same time on a college campus of over 30,000 students. We then met in a Christian group. Otherwise I never would have met her because we had nothing else in common. Each of you can probably think of similar ways your life has been enriched through salvation.

2. God sometimes delivers us from hopeless situations in our lives, and at other times He stands with us as we live through them. But in either case we can rely on these principles:

    a. No trial can ever separate us from God (Rom. 8:31-39).

    b. No crisis will come that we cannot bear with His help (1 Cor. 10:13).

    c. No disaster will occur in which the results cannot be used by God for our good (Rom. 8:28).

## The Answer

Life confronts us with a steady stream of needs and crises. We continually need answers about God, ourselves, and life. In these 12 chapters I have tried to make one central point: the answers to our needs are found in God Himself. He personally touches our lives at the point of our needs. With Him at our side we can face anything.